9408481 FA

IRISH D1643312

Gallery Books
*Editor:* Peter Fallon

A MONTH IN THE COUNTRY

Brian Friel

# A MONTH
# IN THE
# COUNTRY

*after Turgenev*

*with an introductory essay
by the author*

Gallery Books

*A Month in the Country*
is first published
simultaneously in paperback
and in a clothbound edition
on the day of the first production,
4 August 1992.

## The Gallery Press
Loughcrew
Oldcastle
County Meath
Ireland

© Brian Friel 1992

ISBN 1 85235 094 6 (*paperback*)
     1 85235 095 4 (*clothbound*)

The Gallery Press receives financial assistance from An Chomhairle Ealaíon / The Arts Council, Ireland, and acknowledges also the assistance of the Arts Council of Northern Ireland in the publication of this book.

# Preface

Turgenev called *A Month in the Country* a comedy, just as Chekhov called *The Cherry Orchard* and *The Seagull* comedies. They were not formally categorizing these plays, I believe, but wished to indicate their own amused and ironic attitude to their characters and the situations those characters found themselves in. But I think that to call *A Month in the Country* a comedy today is restricting to the play: it imposes a reading on the text and suggests a response to it that could be inhibiting to actors and audience. *A Month in the Country* is certainly not a tragedy. Neither is it a comedy. Perhaps we should settle for 'a play in five scenes'.

I have attributed to the characters the ages given in T. A. Greenan's standard text. But I think that all of those parts could and perhaps should be played by slightly older actors. And I trust I will not offend the purists by tinkering with the Russian names and forms of address.

A literal translation of Turgenev's text was done for me by Christopher Heaney. From it I have composed this very free version. In places it may not be reverent to the original but nowhere, I hope, is it unfaithful to its spirit.

*Brian Friel*

# Ivan Turgenev (1818-1883)

Two years before his death, on one of his compulsive return visits to Russia, Turgenev stopped off at St Petersburg to visit Tolstoy and Sonya at Yasnaya Polyana. The date was August 22, 1881. It was Sonya's birthday. The house was full of guests. Turgenev was then a celebrated writer with a huge — Tolstoy thought inflated — reputation. To the young guests at the party, most of whom had never been beyond Petersburg, he was mesmerising, an exotic: well over six feet, handsome, charming, a bachelor, magnificently dressed, multilingual, in this gathering flamboyantly, even aggressively, European; and of course internationally famous. They questioned him about his work, about London, about literary trends, about his Oxford degree. Their hunger and their awe lured him into garrulity and exaggeration. Avoiding Tolstoy's cold eye he launched into witty stories about the latest fashions in Paris. And then suddenly the sixty-three year old writer jumped to his feet, threw off his gold jacket, stuck his thumbs into his silk waistcoat and gave an exuberant demonstration of the dance that was all the rage on the French vaudeville stage — the cancan. After a few minutes, breathless and exhausted, he collapsed into an armchair.

That night in his diary Tolstoy, younger than Turgenev by ten years but more knowing by a score, commemorated the event — not his wife's birthday but Turgenev's exhibition. He wrote, 'August 22. Turgenev. Sad.'

The entry was tart but off-centre. Turgenev was not sad. He was confused. All his days he was a ditherer, racked between irreconcilable beliefs and compulsions. An instinctive revolutionary who needed the complacency of conservatism. A Slavophile whose heart loved Russia with an intuitive passion but who offered his mind to Europe to mould. A writer who was never sure whether he was a dramatist, a novelist, a poet or an essayist. A bachelor who throughout his entire life loved the married Pauline Viardot faithfully and without reservation — but who fathered a child by a servant-girl and had several casual affairs with discreet women. A dramatist who believed his plays should be read, not performed, and who could not make up his mind whether to call this play *The Student* or *Two Women* or *A Month in the Country*. A sportsman who enjoyed grouse-shooting in Scotland and painting in the south of France but who was always haunted by a sense that real life, a life of content and fulfilment, had somehow eluded him but was available elsewhere, if only he could locate just where.

But for all his vacillations, the inner man, the assured artist, was organised and practical. With what Graham Greene once called 'admirable domestic economy' he marshalled all these irreconcilables and put them to use in his work. Vacillation, the inability to act decisively, the longing to be other, to be elsewhere, became the very core of his dramatic action. He fashioned a new kind of dramatic situation and a new kind of dramatic character where for the first time psychological and poetic elements create a theatre of moods and where the action resides in internal emotion and secret turmoil and not in external events. We now have a name for that kind of drama: we call it Chekhovian. But in *A Month in the Country* Turgenev had written Chekhovian characters and situations forty-six years before Chekhov wrote his first fully Chekhovian play, *The Seagull*.

*A Month in the Country* was first performed at the Maly Theatre in 1872, more than twenty years after it was completed. The newness of its form baffled audiences and critics. Because it eluded classification they called it 'old-fashioned' and 'undramatic'. Turgenev had to wait a further seven years for a new production and a warmer reception. Then came Chekhov a decade later; and the new form was crafted to shimmering perfection. The undramatic became the new drama. And in the years to follow *A Month in the Country* found acceptance in the slipstream of Chekhov's astonishing achievement.

The term metabiosis in chemistry denotes a mode of living in which one organism is dependent on another for the preparation of an environment in which it can live. The relationship between Turgenev and Chekhov was richly metabiotic. *A Month in the Country* was before its time and moved haltingly across unmapped territory. But it established the necessary environment in which Chekhov could blossom. And once Chekhov had achieved

his full stature, once Chekhovian drama was confidently established, the environment was again ready for the reclamation and
reassessment and full understanding of Turgenev's pioneering
work. So they gave life to each other. And between them they
changed the face of European drama.

*Brian Friel*

# Characters

ARKADY SERGEYEVICH ISLAYEV (36), rich landlord
NATALYA PETROVNA (29), his wife
VERA ALEKSANDROVNA (17), Natalya's ward
ANNA SEMYONOVNA ISLAYEVA (58), Arkady's widowed mother
LIZAVETA BOGDANOVNA (37), Anna's companion
HERR SCHAAF (45), German tutor
MICHEL ALEKSANDROVICH RAKITIN (30), family friend
ALEKSEY NIKOLAYEVICH BELYAYEV (21), student/tutor
AFANASY IVANOVICH BOLSHINTSOV (57), neighbouring landowner
IGNATY ILYICH SHPIGELSKY (40), local doctor
MATVEY (43), servant
KATYA (20), servant

## Time and place

The action takes place on the Islayev estate at the beginning of the 1840s. A period of about a day passes between each scene.

## Music

John Field (1782-1837)
No.  5 Nocturne in B-flat major: Andantino
No.  9 Nocturne in E-flat major: Andantino
No. 18 Midi in J. major: Allegretto

*A Month in the Country* was first produced by the Gate Theatre, Dublin, on 4 August 1992, with the following cast:

| | |
|---|---|
| NATALYA | Catherine Byrne |
| ARKADY | Mark Lambert |
| VERA | Karen Ardiff |
| ANNA | Joan O'Hara |
| LIZAVETA | Susan FitzGerald |
| SCHAAF | John Kavanagh |
| MICHEL | Lorcan Cranitch |
| ALEKSEY | J. D. Kelleher |
| BOLSHINTSOV | John Cowley |
| SHPIGELSKY | Donal McCann |
| MATVEY | Mal Whyte |
| KATYA | Antoine Byrne |

| | |
|---|---|
| *Director* | Joe Dowling |
| *Set designer* | Eileen Diss |
| *Costume designer* | Dani Everett |
| *Lighting designer* | Mick Hughes |
| *Music played by* | John O'Conor |
| *Stage director* | Lita O'Connell |
| *Assistant stage managers* | Liz Nugent |
| | Arnold Fanning |

*for Brian B. with love*

# ACT ONE

## Scene One

*Summer afternoon in the early 1840s.*

*The drawing-room in the Islayev home on their remote and wealthy estate. Three doors lead from the drawing-room: one right to the rest of the house; one left to the yard, farm etc.; and one centre to the garden area. (Left and right from the point of view of the audience.)*

*Upstage left three people are playing Preference (a kind of whist) at a large table:* HERR SCHAAF, *the German tutor of Kolya, the ten-year-old son of the house;* ANNA SEMYONOVNA, *the widowed head of the household; and* LIZAVETA BOGDANOVNA, *Anna's companion.*

*Downstage left* NATALYA PETROVNA *(Arkady's wife, Anna's daughter-in-law) is painting. Close to her on a stool sits* MICHEL ALEKSANDROVICH RAKITIN, *a friend of the family. He is staring into the middle-distance. A book hangs between his legs. He is listening inattentively to the music coming from an adjoining room.*

*In the adjoining room* VERA ALEKSANDROVNA, *Natalya's ward, plays a John Field nocturne on the piano — No. 9 in E-flat major.*

SCHAAF *again deals the cards. He then cuts the remainder of the pack and holds up the top card.*

SCHAAF  Hartz are trumpery.

LIZAVETA  *(So anxious to please)* Sorry? Sorry? I —

SCHAAF  Hartz are trumpery.

LIZAVETA  *(To* ANNA*)* I'm afraid I don't under-

ANNA  He means hearts, my dear.

SCHAAF  Ja. Hartz.

LIZAVETA  Ah.

ANNA  The word is trump, Herr Schaaf. Trumpery is a different thing altogether. Trump. Hearts are trump.

SCHAAF  Trump. Danke schön. Hartz are trump. *(Pause)* You come to the front, Lizaveta.

17

LIZAVETA I beg your pardon? (*To* ANNA) What do I do? (*To* SCHAAF) Sorry, I —
SCHAAF You come to the front.
ANNA I think perhaps he means you lead.
SCHAAF You lead. Danke schön.

> KATYA, *demure and knowing, enters with a tray and removes the tea things.*

LIZAVETA Ah, yes — of course — I lead — I lead —
NATALYA (*Softly, with brittle, almost frantic smile*) Dear God — good God — dear, good kind God.

> MICHEL *leans over and squeezes her hand in consolation.*

LIZAVETA Would you like me to lead the four of spades, Madam?
ANNA What I would like, my sweet Lizaveta — (*Controlling herself*) There was a time when playing a game of cards before dinner was one of life's less complex pleasures. (*To* KATYA) And this glass, too, Katya.
KATYA Certainly, Madam.
SCHAAF (*Roguishly*) This tea was gut, Katya.
KATYA I'm glad you enjoyed it.
SCHAAF Schön — sehr schön.
KATYA You're very welcome, Herr Schaaf.
SCHAAF (*To* ANNA) What is Vera play on piano?
ANNA It's a John Field nocturne, isn't it? (*To* NATALYA) Isn't that John Field, Natalya?
NATALYA Is it? I don't know.
ANNA All of a sudden she's a very mature pianist, your little ward.
NATALYA She should be out in the sun. (*To* KATYA) Tell Miss Vera that's enough practice. Go outside and play games or something.
KATYA Yes, Madam.
ANNA I met John Field in Moscow once — shortly after my husband's death; oh, thirty years ago. A very handsome man with that angular Irish face. Have I

told you that story, Herr Schaaf?

SCHAAF And he say to you, 'The most interesting women are widowers.'

ANNA Widows, Herr Schaaf. 'The most interesting women are widows.' There are times when I think your vocabulary is wilfully inadequate. And that's my trick, thank you very much. And now I think I'll try . . . this.

NATALYA Read some more of Mr Sterne to me, Michel. We're at page 115.

MICHEL I thought I was boring you.

NATALYA Of course you're not boring me. Please.

MICHEL 'I have dropped the curtain over this scene for a minute — to remind you of one thing and to inform you of another. What I have to inform you comes, I own, a little out of its due course — for it should have been —'

NATALYA Have you seen Arkady today?

MICHEL At lunch. And this morning down at the dam.

NATALYA Showing off the new sluice-gate he invented?

MICHEL It's a very clever design.

NATALYA Bubbling with energy and enthusiasm?

MICHEL Have you seen it?

NATALYA My energetic husband — the dam enthusiast. Amn't I blessed?

MICHEL Enthusiasm can be a virtue.

NATALYA I think it's a vice.

MICHEL Well of course if it's carried to —

NATALYA Yes, it's a virtue — yes, it's a vice. Don't you know that nothing bores a woman more quickly than an excessive desire to please?

MICHEL So you want me to disagree with whatever you —

NATALYA Oh God, I want — I want — I want — (*Controlling herself and flashing a smile*) I want you to read to me . . . please . . . .

*He spreads his hands and searches for the place in the book.*

ANNA Natalya.

NATALYA Yes?

ANNA Is little Kolya down at the dam with his father?

NATALYA He's out in the garden with his new tutor.

ANNA As long as he has his head covered in that sun.

NATALYA He'll be fine, Grandmother. Stop fussing.

SCHAAF (*To* LIZAVETA) Once again hartz.

LIZAVETA Sorry? (*To* ANNA) Sorry?

SCHAAF Hartz are trumpery once more.

ANNA Why should one battle with fate? Hartz are indeed trumpery and once again you come up to the front, Lizaveta.

LIZAVETA What do you want me to do, Madam?

ANNA Dear, sweet girl, play a card — play any card at all — what does it matter?

LIZAVETA All right. I'll hazard the only heart I have.

ANNA Why not. Hazard away.

MICHEL Your son has a new tutor?

NATALYA Got him a few weeks ago — Aleksey Belyayev. See what happens when your back is turned.

MICHEL Not another randy old goat like Schaaf?

NATALYA He's twenty-one; open; eager; energetic.

MICHEL Handsome?

NATALYA Only just graduated; hungry for the world; and thrilled with himself to have landed a summer job with such exciting people.

MICHEL Enthusiasm — good!

NATALYA You won't like him. He hasn't enough grace for you.

MICHEL He's only twenty-one.

NATALYA And that's why I like him.

MICHEL Because he's graceless or because he's twenty-one?

NATALYA But mostly, I think, because he's so unlike us: he's so . . . unjaded.

MICHEL So this is going to be another day of little needles, is it?

*She takes the book from his hands, leaves it on the floor, and takes his hands affectionately in hers.*

NATALYA No, it's not. I'm sorry, Michel. Just talk to me. Not serious talk — silly talk — chatter — gossip. Tell me about your visit to the Krinistins.

MICHEL Real meaty gossip?

NATALYA The meatier the better.

MICHEL Right. Seven months married and already the Krinistins are bored with one another.

*She withdraws her hands in shock.*

NATALYA Oh God, no! Oh God, that's terrible!

MICHEL Sorry. I shouldn't have —

NATALYA Who told you that? They never admitted that?

MICHEL It was palpable. Bored with each other. Bored with me. And after two days I was bored with them.

NATALYA But you love the Krinistins, Michel.

MICHEL My oldest and closest friends.

NATALYA I don't understand that.

MICHEL That we bored one another? Yes, you do, Natalya. Nobody better.

NATALYA And I won't believe it.

MICHEL That love and boredom aren't perfectly compatible?

NATALYA What does that mean?

MICHEL Maybe even complementary — that's closer to it!

NATALYA I get really angry when you talk like that, Michel. Because you're not talking to me at all: you're playing a private little game of your own. You're like those lace-makers in those gloomy, airless rooms — each one totally isolated, totally concentrated on those minute, complex, subtle little stitches. As if nothing in the world mattered but those ridiculous little stitches.

MICHEL All I suggested was —

NATALYA That's the way we all live here (*everybody in the room*) — making minute, private little stitches. I'm sick of gloomy, airless, constricting rooms.

MICHEL You *are* angry with me today. Has something happened while I was away?

*She looks closely at him for a second; then squeezes his shoulder b iefly.*

NATALYA You are a kind man and a subtle man and a man of great delicacy. But there are times when I think you know nothing about me.

ANNA And since I have no hartz I cross with the seven of clubs. Which gives me — (*Counts*) — four — five — six — seven tricks. And game.

SCHAAF Not game yet.

ANNA Oh, yes. Game now, Herr Schaaf.

SCHAAF (*Very angry, to* LIZAVETA) Why you come forward with spade? You know I have diamond Kaiser!

ANNA Diamond king.

SCHAAF So why you come forward with spade?

LIZAVETA I thought — I don't know — I come forward with spade because I think —

ANNA Please! No post-mortems. Thank you kindly, Herr Schaaf — Lizaveta.

SCHAAF With Lizaveta Bogdanovna ever again I refuse to couple!

LIZAVETA What do you — !

ANNA I think perhaps you mean to partner, Herr Schaaf. To couple is a different . . . My shawl, please, Lizaveta. Time for a breath of air before we eat.

*Suddenly we hear* ALEKSEY BELYAYEV *in the distance.*

ALEKSEY (*Very slowly*) One — two — three — four — five — (*very rapidly*) nineteen-twenty-seven-seventy-six-eighty-four — (*very slowly*) ninety-seven — ninety-eight — ninety-nine — one hundred! Here I come, Kolya!

NATALYA (*To* MICHEL) That's him.

ALEKSEY I can smell you! I will eat you up!

NATALYA The new tutor.

MICHEL He cheats.

NATALYA It's a game, Michel — just a game.

*And suddenly* ALEKSEY BELYAYEV *bursts into the room. He is half-way across the floor before he realises where he is. Now he stops, freezes with embarrassment and looks from one staring face to the other.*

*Nobody rescues him. He begins to withdraw back-wards. As he does:*

ALEKSEY  I'm — I'm sorry — forgive me — Kolya and I — we were playing a game of . . .

ANNA  My grandson's not here, young man. Try the gazebo — that's a favourite hiding-place of his.

ALEKSEY  I'll try that — thank you — I'm really sorry for —

NATALYA  Why are you apologising, Aleksey?

ALEKSEY  Because I — thank you — I'm —

*He hesitates for a second, then suddenly turns and dashes off.*

ANNA  Himself and Kolya together — you would scarcely know which was the pupil.

LIZAVETA  Indeed, it would be hard to tell.

MICHEL  (*To* NATALYA) The new tutor?

NATALYA  Aleksey Belyayev. What do you think?

MICHEL  Seems a fine young man. Maybe a bit . . . un-finished?

NATALYA  We'll finish him, Michel! We'll complete his educa-tion! That'll be our game for the summer: Polish the Tutor!

MICHEL  He interests you, doesn't he?

NATALYA  Interests me?

MICHEL  Does he know he has impressed you?

NATALYA  Michel, he is only a —

MICHEL  He must be very pleased with himself.

NATALYA  I have no idea what he thinks or how he thinks. Nor have you. People like Master Belyayev are altogether different from us. We know nothing about them — we're so busy with our little stitches. Trouble is, for all our — (*She mimes lace-making*) — we know very little about ourselves either. (*She looks at his eager face and tousles his hair*) Just teasing — that's all. And if I can't tease you, who can I tease?

MICHEL  (*Looking around*) Any volunteers?

NATALYA  Because you know what you are to me, Michel.

MICHEL  Tell me again.

NATALYA You know very well. I don't have to say it.

SCHAAF (*To* LIZAVETA) The cat's gone! Who stole the cat? Was it you?

LIZAVETA Cat? What cat?

SCHAAF It was sitting there. Did you stole it?

ANNA Not quite right, Herr Schaaf. The pool of money is called the kitty.

SCHAAF Ah.

ANNA And I took it because I won the last hand.

MATVY *appears at the door.*

MATVEY Excuse me, please — Doctor Shpigelsky has —

*Doctor* SHPIGELSKY *enters.*

DOCTOR He's here, Matvey. How's the arthritis?

MATVEY A lot better, Doctor, thank you. Those pills are great.

DOCTOR Good. Not interrupting, am I? (*Kisses* ANNA'*s hand*) Afternoon, Madam.

ANNA Welcome, Doctor Shpigelsky.

DOCTOR Thank you. And Lizaveta — (*Kisses her hand*) — Well, if we're not elegant today.

LIZAVETA Doctor!

DOCTOR And Herr Schaaf.

SCHAAF Guten Tag.

DOCTOR And the beautiful Natalya Petrovna. (*Kisses her hand*)

NATALYA How are you, Doctor?

DOCTOR How are *you*?

MICHEL Prickly.

DOCTOR No, she's not! (*A parody of taking her pulse*) Oh, *very* fast! But nothing that a good laugh wouldn't cure. Michel, how are you?

MICHEL Managing.

DOCTOR Oh-ho, don't like the sound of *that*.

NATALYA You have the news of the countryside; bring some fresh air in here; cure us all; give us a good laugh.

DOCTOR Right! A laugh . . . a laugh . . . Yes! The station-master told me this one last night. Two farm labourers crawling to work at dawn on Monday morning. One says to the other, 'I am destroyed; I was with this enormously fat woman last night and about five in the morning she caught me by — ' Yes. No, no, that's not funny at all — not a bit. Ever since his wife had those triplets, for some reason that stationmaster has become very coarse . . . .

*Silence.*

In point of fact, the story I did intend telling you was about this man who comes knocking at the doctor's door in the middle of the night. 'Doctor, Doctor, please help me: I'm suffering from very bad amnesia.' 'When did you get this?' 'Get what, Doctor?'

*Again total silence.* LIZAVETA *attempts a polite laugh — it dies too.*

Well, you *did* encourage me.

ANNA You are a solicitous doctor and that's much more important than being an indifferent comedian. (*She gathers her belongings*) Oh, dear; needles in my legs when I sit too long.

NATALYA Then you shouldn't sit too long, should you?

ANNA Indeed . . .

*As she exits — to* SCHAAF:

Trump — lead — widow — kitty. Got those?

SCHAAF Ja. With latitude, Madam.

ANNA With gratitude, Herr Schaaf. One step at a time — no big leaps. (*To* LIZAVETA) I think I'll lie down for a while.

LIZAVETA That's a very good idea.

DOCTOR (*As* LIZAVETA *passes*) Brown suits you.

LIZAVETA It's maroon.

DOCTOR Suits you even better.

*She blushes and exits after* ANNA. SCHAAF *picks up his books.* NATALYA *puts away her painting materials.* SHPIGELSKY *goes to* MICHEL.

        Atmosphere a bit chilly, is it?

MICHEL  Is it?

DOCTOR  Bit edgy, is she (*Natalya*)?

MICHEL  Is she?

DOCTOR  Sorry — sorry — read it wrong again. Herr Schaaf, wie ist Ihres Befinden?

SCHAAF  Wie ist *Ihr* Befinden.

DOCTOR  Ah — Ihr.

SCHAAF  And in my riposte I respond, 'I am vell'.

        *As* SCHAAF *exits:*

DOCTOR  (*To himself*) You are vell. Velly damn good. You make me velly damn happy . . . . Natalya, have you a second?

NATALYA  Yes?

DOCTOR  By ourselves.

NATALYA  Clean those brushes, Michel. (*To* DOCTOR) What is it?

DOCTOR  Somebody I know quite well — a friend actually — a very close friend in fact — he has asked me if I would ask you what — what — what hopes — plans — you have in mind for the wonderful pianist.

NATALYA  The who?

DOCTOR  For your ward. For Vera.

NATALYA  What do you mean — plans?

DOCTOR  Hopes — expectations — aspirations. What this acquaintance — this friend — asked me to ask you is —

NATALYA  He wants to marry her.

        *Brief pause.*

DOCTOR  Nail on head.

NATALYA  You're really joking now, Doctor Shpigelsky.

DOCTOR  Deadly serious.

NATALYA  Your acquaintance — your closest friend — wants to
marry Vera!

DOCTOR  A very genuine proposal.

NATALYA  Vera's a child, Doctor!

DOCTOR  My friend suggests that —

NATALYA  She's barely seventeen!

DOCTOR  Nowadays young ladies of seventeen are —

NATALYA  And who is this close friend?

DOCTOR  Now — now — please — please — one step at a time.
And when you think it over, you may see that —

*He breaks off because* VERA *runs on — an entrance
like* ALEKSEY's. *Her face is flushed and animated.*

NATALYA  (*In admonition*) Doctor!

*He puts his finger to his lips and smiles at her.*

VERA  (*To* MICHEL) Have you any glue — or paste — or
sticky stuff of any sort?

MICHEL  (*Feeling his pockets*) Certainly have, Vera. Never move
without it.

VERA  You are a clown, Michel!

MICHEL  What is it for?

VERA  Aleksey and I are making a kite. Well, Aleksey is.
For Kolya.

MICHEL  (*Leaving*) Leave it to Michel.

*He exits.*

NATALYA  Aren't you saying hello to Doctor Shpigelsky, Vera?

VERA  Hello, Doctor.

DOCTOR  How are you, young lady?

NATALYA  Can't you see how she is? Look at those shoes! What
in God's name have you been doing, child?

VERA  We were down at the dam. You should see the new
sluice-gates Arkady designed — they're wonderful.
Then we played rounders on the old tennis court.
Aleksey's a great runner and he —

NATALYA  Aleksey Belyayev's our new tutor.

VERA  And now we're making a kite. Aleksey can make a Chinese box-kite.

*MICHEL returns.*

MICHEL  This one lasts a day. This one lasts forever. (*To* NATALYA) Which one should she take?
NATALYA  Just give her some glue, Michel.
VERA  Can I have them both?
MICHEL  Certainly can.

*VERA kisses him quickly.*

VERA  You're great. Thanks. We'll probably use the forever stuff.
NATALYA  Careful in that sun, child.
DOCTOR  And I have a patient to see. And I've never seen a Chinese box-kite. (*To* VERA) May I watch?
NATALYA  (*In admonition again*) Doctor!

*Again he puts his finger to his lips as he exits with* VERA.

DOCTOR  Ze velly soul of discletion.

*As soon as they leave* MICHEL *takes* NATALYA *in his arms from behind.*

MICHEL  Something's wrong.
NATALYA  Nothing's wrong now.
MICHEL  Talk to me about it.

*He turns her to face him.*

NATALYA  I'm so restless, so irritable all day. But I'm fine now. Why are you searching my face like that?
MICHEL  Just to look at you is a great . . . happiness.
NATALYA  You are the kindest man in the world —
MICHEL  Natalya —
NATALYA  — and the most gentle and the most considerate

and the most understanding. And you're so . . .
permanent. What would I do without you?

MICHEL Only you know the answer to that.

NATALYA When I'm with you I feel so centred. Just to be with
you — this is the only happiness I want. I mean that
with all my heart.

MICHEL Beautiful Natalya.

NATALYA Hundreds of women would envy me, wouldn't
they?

MICHEL Thousands! Millions!

NATALYA Oh, yes, they would. To be loved by such a good
man? Oh, yes, that must be enviable. Strange, isn't
it?

MICHEL I don't know what's strange any more. I just know I
am in love with you.

NATALYA And I love you, too.

MICHEL Do you?

NATALYA Yes, I do. You know I love you. And the moment I
say that, the moment I make that acknowledgement,
I think . . .

MICHEL Go on.

NATALYA I think: that man has never made me suffer; that
man has never made me cry; and if I have never
cried because of him, I can't really love him, can I?
Sounds ridiculous, doesn't it? Is it ridiculous?

MICHEL Maybe not.

NATALYA Probably is. I don't know. How long have we known
each other?

MICHEL Years and years and years.

NATALYA That makes us old friends, doesn't it?

MICHEL Is that what we are?

NATALYA But it does, doesn't it? We *are* friends, aren't we?

MICHEL Let's talk about something else, Natalya. The little
shred of happiness I cling to, I feel it slipping away
from me.

ARKADY ISLAYEV's *voice off:*

ARKADY Tell him to keep the water at that level, Matvey.

MATVEY (*Off*) Yessir.

NATALYA  Arkady. I can't face him now.

MICHEL  Natalya —

NATALYA  (*Leaving*) Not just at the moment. I'll be straight back.

ARKADY  (*Off*) And we'll not open the gates until the water rises another six inches. (*He enters*) Ah, Michel! And how are you today, Michel? Are you well?

MICHEL  We had lunch together, Arkady.

ARKADY  Had we? Cold partridge! — Of course we had! And we agreed we both prefer partridge to grouse. (*Searching through drawers of cabinet*) Where did I leave . . . ? (*Finds document*) Ah! (*To* MICHEL) The Russian workman never fails to astonish me, Michel. You see that group of men I have down at the weir? As bright and as keen a group of men you could ask for, *provided* — and maybe this is characteristic of the Russian psyche at every level of society — provided you lead them with intelligence but especially with authority — where's Natalya?

MICHEL  She was around a moment ago.

ARKADY  But leave them for ten minutes without that leadership and — (*Claps his hands once*) — chaos! Astonishing, isn't it?

MICHEL  Is the new dam nearly finished?

ARKADY  This is what I want — I think. Not to be pedantic, Michel, it's a weir, not a dam. And yes, it's almost complete. Why are you laughing at me?

MICHEL  Just smiling at the way you —

ARKADY  Yes, I suppose I am slightly . . . what am I?

MICHEL  I was smiling because you —

ARKADY  Yes, I always seem to be simultaneously very busy and very confused, don't I? Yes, I'm not unaware of that. But there was a time — oh, long before you and I became friends — oh, yes, there was a time, strange as it may seem — when — when I was as busy but much, much less confused. Ivan hasn't been here?

MICHEL  Who?

ARKADY  That new tutor Natalya found somewhere. Ivan something.

MICHEL  Isn't his name Aleksey?

ARKADY  Whatever. I gave him a simple errand to do and I'm afraid he's —

*ALEKSEY enters.*

Just asking about you, young man. You left the grease-gun with the foreman?

ALEKSEY  Yes. And now he wants the plans with the blue ribbon.

ARKADY  The blue — the blue — the blue —   Here we are. That's blue, isn't it? (*Handing the document over*) Good man. You two know each other, don't you?

MICHEL  We haven't actually spoken to one another.

ARKADY  Ah. Michel Rakitin — Ivan — sorry — Aleksey Belyayev. Why do I keep calling you Ivan? Anyhow. Master Belyayev is teaching our Kolya — what *are* you teaching him?

ALEKSEY  French and English.

ARKADY  Exactly — French and English.

*NATALYA enters.*

Ah, Natalya! You look just astonishing. Doesn't my astonishing wife look just . . . astonishing? Give me a kiss. Ah. And guess what has arrived.

NATALYA  What?

ARKADY  Guess.

NATALYA  How can I guess, Arkady?

ARKADY  The new winnowing-machine! Outside in the yard! And it is just astonishing. Come out and see it.

NATALYA  I don't understand those machines of yours, Arkady. Michel will go with you.

MICHEL  Yes!

ARKADY  You don't understand machines either, Michel, do you? Doesn't matter. Just to look at this thing is an unqualified pleasure. Astonishing!

*ARKADY and MICHEL leave together. ALEKSEY moves to follow them.*

NATALYA  Where are you going?

ALEKSEY  I've got to give this to —

NATALYA  Sit there. You're almost a month here and we haven't had a chance to talk. (*Points to chair*) There.

*He sits stiffly.*

Have we?

ALEKSEY  Have we — ?

NATALYA  Talked.

ALEKSEY  Oh. Yes — yes — no — no.

NATALYA  I make you uneasy for some reason. Are your parents alive?

ALEKSEY  My mother died when I was a baby.

NATALYA  Your father?

ALEKSEY  He's still alive.

NATALYA  Brothers and sisters?

ALEKSEY  One sister.

NATALYA  Are you and she close?

ALEKSEY  We are even though —

NATALYA  What's her name?

ALEKSEY  Natalya.

NATALYA  That's my name.

ALEKSEY  Is it?

NATALYA  Natalya.

ALEKSEY  It's a nice name.

NATALYA  You like it?

ALEKSEY  It's her name, too — my sister's. Natalya.

NATALYA  You've already told me that. Do you love your sister?

ALEKSEY  We're very close.

NATALYA  How do you find Kolya?

ALEKSEY  Great. He's bright and quick and —

NATALYA  He thinks you're wonderful. Every night before he goes to sleep he tells me everything you've done together during the day. I think he loves you. Were you and your father close?

ALEKSEY  (*Laughs*) My father never looked near us. He was a sort of itinerant labourer — went wherever the work was. And never sober. Natalya and I, we were — I suppose — dragged up by neighbours.

NATALYA You sing very well.

ALEKSEY Me!

NATALYA I heard you in the garden.

ALEKSEY God! When?

NATALYA Yesterday evening.

ALEKSEY Oh my God!

NATALYA One of these days, when we get to know each other a lot better, you'll sing a song for me.

ALEKSEY I really can't —

NATALYA You won't sing for me?

ALEKSEY It's not that I won't — it's just that I —

NATALYA So you will.

ALEKSEY Honest to God, I'm terrible!

NATALYA But you will, Aleksey — won't you?

ALEKSEY If you insist, then —

NATALYA Just one song. That's not a lot to ask, is it? Will you do that? For me?

> *She holds her hand to him. He takes it. Then in a moment of confusion and warmth kisses it.* NATALYA *quickly withdraws it. At the moment of the kiss* DOCTOR SHPIGELSKY *enters. There is general embarrassment. Then* SHPIGELSKY *speaks rapidly.*

DOCTOR Just had a look at old Ivan, the blacksmith . . . You know, while I was in the house . . . two birds — one stone . . . Ninety if he's a day, old Ivan . . . (*To* ALEKSEY) Shpigelsky, local G.P. And you're the new tutor. Watched you making a kite out there. Anyhow, at death's door last Saturday, Ivan. But today? Sitting at the kitchen table, knocking back vodka and stuffing himself with pancakes. The doctor's dilemma, young man: if you cure nobody, you're never sent for — consequently no income. Cure everybody, you end up with no patients — consequently no income. What's the solution?

ALEKSEY If you'll excuse me, I've to give this to the foreman.

NATALYA That can wait. We're about to eat and —

> VERA *runs on and goes straight to* ALEKSEY.

VERA Come on, Aleksey! We're waiting for you! What's keeping you? Kolya wants you to attach the tail.

NATALYA Calm down, child. What's all the excitement?

VERA Kolya sent me up for Aleksey. (*To* ALEKSEY) Where have you been?

NATALYA *adjusts* VERA's *dress and hair.*

NATALYA Look at the mess you're in. What way is that collar? That's better. Now. We're going to eat. Are you staying the night, Doctor?

DOCTOR May I?

NATALYA You're welcome.

DOCTOR Love to. My old horse is as wheezy as myself. Love to. Thank you.

VERA *and* ALEKSEY *have been whispering and laughing together.*

VERA Just as the swing was at its height, off she came like a ton of bricks.

ALEKSEY Nanny!

VERA Flat on her big fat bottom!

ALEKSEY She did not! Great!

VERA Made a huge crater in the ground!

ALEKSEY Too good for her!

VERA 'Help me! My back's broken!'

NATALYA What's this? Did somebody have an accident?

VERA Nanny fell off the swing.

NATALYA What was Nanny doing on the swing?

VERA Swinging.

NATALYA Vera, please. Was she hurt?

VERA Only her bottom.

VERA *and* ALEKSEY *laugh again.*

NATALYA That swing is dangerous, Aleksey.

ALEKSEY No, it's safe now. I fixed it this morning.

NATALYA Nobody is to play on it again.

ALEKSEY But it's quite —

NATALYA Nobody. Is that understood?

ALEKSEY Yes.

NATALYA You two go ahead into the dining-room. We'll join you in a minute.

VERA *and* ALEKSEY *exit.*

NATALYA Hand me that (*paint*) box, Doctor. About that suggestion of yours.

DOCTOR Suggestion?

NATALYA Your proposition — your friend's proposal.

DOCTOR Ah! About Vera and —

NATALYA Yes. About Vera. Let me think about that, Doctor.

DOCTOR For as long as you like.

NATALYA Yes, I'll give that some thought.

DOCTOR Good.

NATALYA And then perhaps we'll talk.

*She offers him her arm and they go out to the dining-room. End of Scene One.*

# ACT ONE

## Scene Two

*The following day. A garden adjoining the house. A birch tree, a gazebo, a garden seat.*

*From the distance the sound of Kolya doing five-finger exercises on the piano.*

*KATYA is on the stage. Bed sheets on the grass. She is folding them and putting them into a laundry basket. As she does she sings.*

> KATYA 'There are many . . . ' etc.
> MATVEY (*Off, softly*) Katya? . . . Katya?

> *She picks up the sheets and dashes into the gazebo.*
> *MATVEY enters.*

> MATVEY (*Urgently, nervously*) Katya? Are you here? Katya, I just want to — You're hiding on me! Why are you hiding on me?
> KATYA I'm working, Matvey. Can't you see?
> MATVEY We've got to talk, Katya.
> KATYA Have we?
> MATVEY Yes — yes — yes! (*His arm around her*) You've changed, Katya. What has happened to you?
> KATYA You're hurting me.
> MATVEY Sorry. (*Releases her*) Something has happened. Did I do something? Say something? Why do you keep avoiding me now?
> KATYA Now?
> MATVEY Yes — now! There was a time when you were — when I thought you were —
> KATYA When you jumped to certain alarming conclusions, Matvey.

MATVEY  I'm crazy about you, Katya. You know I am.

KATYA  When you made certain distressing assumptions you had no right to make.

MATVEY  At the dance — and that's only a month ago — you told me that —

KATYA  That I enjoyed your company — on occasion — for brief periods.

MATVEY  Oh God, Katya love, please —

KATYA  We have discussed you at length on several occasions.

MATVEY  Who has?

KATYA  Mother and I.

MATVEY  What does that mean?

KATYA  She says that the gap between our ages — actually the word she used was 'chasm' — it is so large —

MATVEY  I'm only forty-three!

KATYA  And so disquieting —

MATVEY  I'm full of vigour!

KATYA  Indeed so unbridgeable that the possibility of a permanent and a mutually fulfilling relationship between us is — again to use her own word — 'pale'.

MATVEY  If your bloody mother would —

KATYA  Careful!

MATVEY  If we were left alone, Katya —

KATYA  So her advice to me is to give my consideration to gentlemen who are closer to me in years and in temperament and in spiritual disposition.

MATVEY  (*Shocked, awed at this*) Jesus Christ!

KATYA  And the curious thing is she likes you.

MATVEY  I never met the woman in my life, Katya!

KATYA  Well, what she knows about you — what I've told her. Every weekend she enquires about your rheumatism.

MATVEY  You told her about that?

KATYA  Her prediction is that within three years you'll be crippled and — (*She breaks off*) Careful — there's the Hun.

*Enter* SCHAAF *with a fishing rod.*

MATVEY Damn the Hun!

KATYA Move! Do you want us both sacked!

MATVEY Katya —

KATYA Move!

*Distraught and irresolute,* MATVEY *dashes off.* SCHAAF's *face lights up when he sees* KATYA. *He is ponderously coquettish.*

SCHAAF Ah! The beautiful Katya! This is my ravishing!

KATYA (*Sweetly*) Hello, Adam.

SCHAAF Observe — I go to apprehend fish. (*Grabs her*) But first I apprehend the beautiful Katya. Come with me.

KATYA Adam, please —

SCHAAF Yes, yes; like last Friday we make lust again beside the lake?

KATYA (*Afraid of being overheard*) For goodness sake, Adam!

SCHAAF I sing a German song to you:
'Kathrinchen, Kathrinchen, wie lieb' ich dich so sehr!'

KATYA My mother says your songs are lascivious.

SCHAAF Yes? Gut — gut! And in Russian that is, 'O Katya, you are so beautiful, and I love you!'

KATYA Somebody's coming. (*Gathers her laundry*) Later perhaps?

SCHAAF Yes? We lust later?

KATYA Adam, you're shameless.

SCHAAF (*Delighted*) So my Mama say, too! Danke — Danke.

KATYA I'm free after dinner.

*She dashes off.* ALEKSEY *enters carrying the tail of the box-kite.* SCHAAF *greets him coldly and with a formal bow.*

SCHAAF Guten Abend.

ALEKSEY Guten Abend, Herr Schaaf.

*Now* VERA, *holding the end of the tail of the kite,*

*enters. And again* SCHAAF *bows formally.*

SCHAAF  Guten Abend, Fräulein.
VERA  Guten Abend, Herr Schaaf.

SCHAAF *exits.* ALEKSEY *dances round the garden, parodying Schaaf's bow and accent and manner. At first* VERA *laughs; then she joins in.*

ALEKSEY  Guten Abend.
VERA  Guten Abend.
ALEKSEY  Guten Abend, I'm a dandy. Guten Abend — also randy.
VERA  Guten Abend, you're so agile.
ALEKSEY  Body agile, brain more fragile. Do you know I'm Kolya's tutor?
VERA  And perhaps young Katya's suitor?
ALEKSEY  Danke — Danke! I'm so flatter.
VERA  Go catch some fish. That's all that matter.
ALEKSEY  Guten Abend.
VERA  Guten Abend.

*They collapse laughing on the bench seat.*

ALEKSEY  I don't trust that man from here to the door.

VERA *jumps to her feet and looks around anxiously.*

VERA  The door? — What door? — Where's the door? — I see no door.

*He grabs her and pulls her back on to the seat.*

ALEKSEY  Don't you be smart with me, Madam. Just hold that (*kite*).
VERA  I can't see you now.

ALEKSEY *makes some last adjustments.*

ALEKSEY  What do you mean?

VERA I can't see what you're doing.

ALEKSEY *lowers the kite.*

I can now. Listen.

*The five-finger exercises have begun again.*

Kolya.
ALEKSEY Lizaveta's a bloody sadist, keeping the child stuck at a piano on a day like this.
VERA I played for an hour this morning.
ALEKSEY You like it. He hates it — he told me.
VERA I'm sure she'd rather be outside, too.
ALEKSEY I don't trust her either. She's too sweet.
VERA She's all right. She fancies you.

*He grabs her in mock anger.*

ALEKSEY You just watch yourself! (*Furtive look around — then whispers in her ear*) Next time you're close to her, look at —

*He runs his index finger across his upper lip.*

VERA Lizaveta has *not* got a moustache, Aleksey.
ALEKSEY Snuff.
VERA What?
ALEKSEY Little thin snuff line.
VERA God forgive you.
ALEKSEY Bright mustard.
VERA Aleksey!
ALEKSEY And look — so have I. (*He thrusts his mouth towards her face*) Where she kissed me this morning.
VERA God forgive you!

*Again horse-play and laughter.*

ALEKSEY Careful. You're going to break the kite. I hope this string's strong enough.

VERA  Do you fly kites in Moscow?

ALEKSEY  My dear child, in Moscow my life is dedicated to scholarship.

VERA  Are you very clever?

ALEKSEY  Genius.

VERA  Really. Are you clever?

ALEKSEY  For God's sake! I barely scraped through my finals! You were at school in Moscow, weren't you?

VERA  Until last year. Until Natalya took me away.

ALEKSEY  Why did she do that?

VERA  For company here, I suppose.

ALEKSEY  Hasn't she a husband? And a mother-in-law? And a house full of servants? That was selfish of her.

VERA  No, it wasn't.

ALEKSEY  Interrupting a brilliant academic career?

*Again she pushes him playfully.*

VERA  Aleksey Belyayev, you are one huge clown!

ALEKSEY  You like Natalya, don't you?

VERA  I love Natalya.

ALEKSEY  Yes, I think you do.

VERA  You sound surprised.

ALEKSEY  All the same you're just a little bit wary of her, aren't you?

VERA  Am I? I don't think I am. (*Pause*) What do you think of her?

ALEKSEY  (*His response is considered*) I have never been inside a grand house like this — ever in my life. I've never met anybody like her — ever in my life. She . . . she astonishes me.

VERA  Does that mean you like her?

ALEKSEY  It means that I am . . . a bit in awe of all this and a bit bewildered by her. (*Casual again*) You're really a daughter to her, aren't you, Baby Face?

VERA  She and Arkady are the only parents I've ever known. You know I'm an orphan, don't you?

ALEKSEY  Yes. I'm half an orphan. My mother's dead.

VERA  They say orphans are often drawn to each other; that there's a natural affinity. What do you think?

ALEKSEY  Irresistibly. Absolutely no doubt about that. This tail is supposed to be ten times the length of the side. Doesn't look long enough to me.

VERA  You have a sister?

ALEKSEY  Another Natalya.

VERA  What age is she?

ALEKSEY  She must be — oh — sixteen — seventeen.

VERA  Are we alike at all?

ALEKSEY  She's only a baby still. And you're far better looking.

VERA  I'm sure.

ALEKSEY  Honestly. And much more sophisticated.

*Pause.*

VERA  I wish I were in her place.

ALEKSEY  You've never seen our house!

VERA  What I meant was —

ALEKSEY  It's so small you've got to go sideways in the front door.

*She laughs and pushes him again.*

Swear to God! And the kitchen's so tiny we take turns to sit in it. (*Another push*) Hi, that was sore! I'm warning you: make sure you marry like Natalya — into big money and a grand house and you'll be happy for the rest of your days.

VERA  Promise?

ALEKSEY  Hope to die. Who wants to sit in a tiny kitchen all day — alone?

*She laughs. The kite is finished.*

ALEKSEY  Now. All we need is a wind to lift it and a boy to fly it. (*Listens*) He's stopped. Let's see if Mustard Lips has released him.

VERA  Here's Natalya and Michel.

ALEKSEY  Will we show them our handiwork?

VERA  Not now. We'll go. She'll only find some reason for

scolding me.

*As they go off:*

ALEKSEY Why would she do that?
VERA Because she's cranky these days.
ALEKSEY Told you you were a little bit wary of her.

MICHEL *and* NATALYA *enter.*

MICHEL Did you see that? Ran off as soon as they spotted us!
NATALYA She spends far too much time with that young man.
MICHEL That was a bit obvious, wasn't it?
NATALYA And she's still only a child.
MICHEL Seventeen.
NATALYA (*Touching the bench*) It's still warm — where they were sitting.
MICHEL Hot young blood, Natalya.
NATALYA I'm going to have a word with her.
MICHEL Don't tell me you envy them?
NATALYA For God's sake, why should I envy them?
MICHEL Their youth? Their freshness? Their vitality?
NATALYA I'm not quite senile yet, Michel.
MICHEL I suppose I should envy them, too. Trouble is, I don't feel old; I don't feel any age. See those two trees, Natalya? That huge oak at the peak of its vigour and maturity. And beside it — look — that slender young birch, so delicate it may well break under next winter's snows. Yet each has its own perfection. Each is replete in itself — isn't it?
NATALYA You are so eloquent about 'nature', Michel; so sensitive, so responsive to it. 'Nature' must be flattered.
MICHEL Oh, yes; thrilled.

KATYA *enters with another basket of laundry.*

NATALYA But of course you're wrong about 'nature'. Nature is blunt and crude and relentless. Nature cares about nothing except itself — surviving and perpetuating itself. Your exquisite nature is a savage. Busy,

43

Katya?

KATYA Kept going, Madam. Would you like me to get you your parasol?

NATALYA I'm fine, thank you, Katya.

KATYA *exits.*

Another delicate young birch, Michel?

MICHEL The word nature will never cross my lips again.

NATALYA Will it break under the winter snows?

MICHEL Not that one. That's a tough birch. That's a surviving birch.

NATALYA Most young birches are.

MICHEL By the way the doctor has left. He says to thank you for the hospitality.

NATALYA Where has he gone?

MICHEL To do some calls. Have you noticed — himself and Lizaveta seem to have got friendly. Whatever it was he was whispering to her at breakfast she was breaking her sides.

NATALYA What a mask! — The genial country doctor!

MICHEL He's all right, Shpigelsky.

NATALYA He's a huckster.

MICHEL He's not.

NATALYA A mean-minded, ugly-minded, conniving peasant.

MICHEL Natalya, that's — !

NATALYA Will he be back soon?

MICHEL Said he would.

NATALYA Something I wanted to talk to him about.

MICHEL What was that? Sorry — none of my —

NATALYA Don't you know?

MICHEL None of my business.

NATALYA But you do know, don't you?

MICHEL How could I possibly — ?

NATALYA You gaze at me all the time, don't you? You know every thought in my head — don't you? You analyse everything I think, everything I do — don't you?

MICHEL You should have your parasol.

NATALYA Don't tell me there's a little portion of my mind that you haven't invaded?

MICHEL  Natalya —

NATALYA  Because if there is, then for all your attentions, for all
your scrutiny, you're not nearly as penetrating as I
thought you were.

MICHEL  Something has happened to you, Natalya.

NATALYA  Another brilliant perception?

MICHEL  I don't know what it is. All I know is that since I've
come back, you've . . . altered. I know — I know —
not at all brilliant. But it is obvious, even to me, that
for some reason you are deeply unhappy within
yourself. And I want you to know that that makes
me deeply unhappy, too. And if there is anything I
can do, anything at all . . . I don't have to tell you
that.

NATALYA  What do you think of Bolshintsov?

MICHEL  Of who?

NATALYA  Bolshintsov! Afanasy Ivanovich Bolshintsov! Who
lives fifteen miles north of here! You know? — Our
neighbour, Bolshintsov!

MICHEL  Of course I know. But —

NATALYA  Tell me about him.

MICHEL  You know him a lot better than I do. Didn't you tell
me he was here playing cards a few weeks ago?

NATALYA  Talk about him.

MICHEL  Bachelor; large, run-down estate; thick; probably
illiterate; an idiot but no fool; cunning — for God's
sake what is there to say about Bolshintsov!

NATALYA  He's not thick.

MICHEL  Who cares? So I'm wrong again.

NATALYA  And he's not illiterate.

MICHEL  Wonderful.

NATALYA  And the estate isn't neglected.

MICHEL  And I'm sure he's charming and entertaining and
industrious. What's the sudden interest in Bolshintsov?

NATALYA  None. Nothing. Just wanted to hear your astute
character analysis.

MICHEL  Natalya —

NATALYA  And now it's time to decide on the dinner menu.
That sun *is* hot. I think we'll have lamb this evening.

MICHEL    Will I go with you?

NATALYA  No, we've had a surfeit of one another, haven't we?
         Well, a sufficiency for now.

> *She exits. The moment she leaves,* MICHEL's *façade of
> calm, of control, suddenly collapses. He is a man on
> the edge of panic. He conducts the following conver-
> sation with himself at a frantic speed.*

MICHEL   Oh my God.
         Steady, man.
         She's slipping away from you.
         No, she's not.
         You're losing her.
         Shut up.
         And if you lose her —
         *I will not lose her!*
         — you lose whatever happiness you know.
         You call this happiness?
         I'm talking about your life. Lose her — lose your life.
         You know that, don't you? But then she has never
         really loved you.
         That's not true!
         Affection, maybe; but it never exploded into love.
         And why is she giving you hell now? It's the young
         tutor, isn't it?
         Infatuation; that will pass.
         Will it?
         Of course it will. She's much too sophisticated for
         that — that calf.
         Perhaps.
         Oh my God.
         Why are you lamenting?
         Because it's out of my hands, altogether beyond my
         control. And all I can do is watch — and endure.
         You're besotted by her, aren't you?
         Yes, I am besotted by her.
         If you could only see yourself: you are ridiculous.
         Ever since the first day I met her I've never been
         anything else.

NATALYA, *now smiling and animated, enters, leading* ALEKSEY *by the elbow. He is flushed — and slightly embarrassed.*

NATALYA I'm telling you — Michel will know. Michel's a very perceptive man. Aren't you, Michel?

MICHEL Michel will know what?

NATALYA Where Aleksey can get gunpowder —

MICHEL (*Icy*) In the town.

NATALYA Yes. But where in the town?

MICHEL What's the mystery, Natalya? You buy gunpowder in Kafinsky's every year, don't you?

NATALYA (*To* ALEKSEY) So we'll buy it in Kafinsky's. Thank you, Michel.

MICHEL (*To* ALEKSEY) You're going to make an explosion?

NATALYA An explosion! Michel!

ALEKSEY Fireworks.

MICHEL Sorry?

ALEKSEY Only fireworks. Just fireworks.

NATALYA (*To* ALEKSEY) Go on — tell him.

ALEKSEY And I need some gunpowder —

MICHEL That much I've gathered.

ALEKSEY Not good quality gunpowder — really cheap gunpowder will do —

NATALYA He's too modest to say it himself but Aleksey can make rockets and Roman candles and Chinese squibs.

MICHEL And fishing rods.

NATALYA And fishing rods.

MICHEL And kites.

NATALYA Which we're going to fly in a few minutes.

MICHEL You're a very accomplished young man.

ALEKSEY It's very easy to —

NATALYA Of course he is. (*To* ALEKSEY) Acknowledge it. Wonderfully accomplished. (*To* MICHEL) And do you know what he's going to do next Thursday night?

MICHEL Tell me.

NATALYA On Thursday of next week?

MICHEL Your birthday — I know.

NATALYA You remembered! (*To* ALEKSEY) Told you — he knows

47

everything. (*To* MICHEL) On Thursday of next week we're going to celebrate my birthday with a fireworks display! At night! Out in the middle of the lake! Aleksey can make fireworks that float on water! Won't that be exciting?

*Enter* SHPIGELSKY *and* BOLSHINTSOV. BOLSHINTSOV *is excited and nervous and smiling resolutely.*

Look who's here. I thought you were out on calls?

DOCTOR I've cured everybody. So once again I'll be broke.

NATALYA And Mr Bolshintsov. Welcome.

*He bows gauchely.*

BOLSHINTSOV Thank you. The doctor brought me with him. And now, since I'm here — Madam, you know me —

NATALYA Yes?

BOLSHINTSOV I'm not a man of much style or grace. So if I can come straight to the point, I'm here because I want —

*The* DOCTOR *grabs him by the arm.*

DOCTOR I told you, Bolshintsov, I know where it is; I'm bringing you there. (*Confidentially to the others*) Taken unawares, saving your delicate presence — chill in the kidneys — very embarrassed. (*Aloud*) Everything under control in a manner of speaking. This way, man; straight ahead. Back in a minute.

NATALYA We're about to launch Kolya's new kite. You'll join us, Doctor?

DOCTOR Wouldn't miss it for the world.

*The* DOCTOR *pushes* BOLSHINTSOV *off.*

NATALYA You know, when he's dressed up, he's quite a handsome man, Bolshintsov, isn't he? Now. (*To* ALEKSEY) Kafinsky's — you'll remember that? Anyhow I'll send Matvey with you and charge whatever you need to my account. There was something else we had to look at — what was it?

ALEKSEY  Kolya's progress report.

NATALYA  That's it. You're fashioning Kolya, and Michel and I
are polishing —

*She looks to include* MICHEL. *But he has drifted
upstage and stands with his back to them. For a few
seconds she looks at him, isolated, wretched. Instinctively she goes to him. She raises her hands as if to put
them consolingly on his shoulders. Then she glances
back at* ALEKSEY *and gives a short uneasy laugh.
Quickly she turns and joins him.*

There are times when Michel prefers to be alone.

*She holds her hand out to him. Just as he is about to
take it:*

No, no, not my hand, Master Tutor.

ALEKSEY  Sorry, I —

NATALYA  Not unless I offer it to you. You take my arm. Taking
my hand would signify something different. And
that could be altogether misleading.

*They exit. For a few seconds* MICHEL *is alone on the
stage. Then the* DOCTOR *and* BOLSHINTSOV *return.*

BOLSHINTSOV  Tell me again —

DOCTOR  (*Wearily*) Bolshintsov!

BOLSHINTSOV  Just once more — what *exactly* did Natalya say?

DOCTOR  'I don't know Mr Bolshintsov very well — '

BOLSHINTSOV  That's right — she doesn't.

DOCTOR  'But he seems a decent sort of man — '

BOLSHINTSOV  That's true — I am.

DOCTOR  'And if he wishes to come and see Vera here — '

BOLSHINTSOV  She meant here — in this house?

DOCTOR  Are you going to let me finish?

BOLSHINTSOV  Sorry.

DOCTOR  'If he wishes to see Vera here in this house, I will
have no objection. Indeed, if he wins her affection — '

BOLSHINTSOV  Wins her affection!

DOCTOR  'I will be the first to congratulate them both.'

BOLSHINTSOV  (*Elated*) Oh God! Those are her very words?

DOCTOR  Hand on heart.

BOLSHINTSOV  (*Dejected*) Oh God! What will I say to her? I won't be able to get a word out. Let me tell you a secret, Doctor: never once in my life — never once have I ever . . . been with a girl, ever.

DOCTOR  You're not serious!

BOLSHINTSOV  So I have no idea how to acquit myself, how to speak, what to say. Maybe I should be very formal, very dignified — what do you say? No, better to be witty, wouldn't it? Yes, that's the tack — witty and debonair — a bit of a lad. Oh God, guide me through this, Doctor, and as well as the three horses I've promised you —

DOCTOR  (*In case they are overheard*) Please!

MICHEL *moves off.*

BOLSHINTSOV  I'll give you a wagonette as well. Guide me, friend.

DOCTOR  The wagonette is new?

BOLSHINTSOV  Never on the road.

DOCTOR  And the horses?

BOLSHINTSOV  Magnificent bays.

DOCTOR  I'm your guide. Let's assess what we have. For God's sake, straighten up, man! What age are you?

BOLSHINTSOV  What has that got to — ? Fifty-seven.

DOCTOR  Size of farm?

BOLSHINTSOV  Five hundred acres, give or take a —

DOCTOR  Serfs?

BOLSHINTSOV  Three hundred and twenty.

DOCTOR  Your social graces. Do you play chess?

BOLSHINTSOV  No, but I'm a devil at snap!

DOCTOR  God! Travel?

BOLSHINTSOV  Moscow every autumn — for the pig-market.

DOCTOR  Music?

BOLSHINTSOV  What do you mean?

DOCTOR  What instruments do you play?

BOLSHINTSOV  When I was a boy I played the mouth-organ.

DOCTOR Christ! Dance?

BOLSHINTSOV Me!

DOCTOR Sorry. Languages?

BOLSHINTSOV Russian.

DOCTOR Brilliant. I have to tell you, it's bleak, Bolshintsov. (*Groping around frantically*) Those are your own teeth, are they?

BOLSHINTSOV Yes! Have them all!

BOLSHINTSOV *pulls his lips apart in pride.*

DOCTOR (*With distaste*) Right — right — right — right — right. Now. Our assets are the following — For God's sake, shut your mouth, Bolshintsov! Property — substantial. Health — excellent. Appearance — presentable. Widely travelled. Fluent linguist — in our native language. Proficient organist — of the mouth. Money in the bank?

BOLSHINTSOV (*Barely audible*) A little.

DOCTOR Didn't get that?

BOLSHINTSOV A little.

DOCTOR How much?

BOLSHINTSOV I wouldn't tell my mother that, Shpigelsky! Enough — just say enough.

DOCTOR With regard to the opposite sex, chaste to a saintly degree.

BOLSHINTSOV That's bad, is it?

DOCTOR No; but in my experience of this whole province — unique. And my job is to make you sound perfectly . . . normal.

BOLSHINTSOV It's the words, Doctor, the words! What am I going to *say* to her? Because if I can't speak, how can I propose to her?

DOCTOR What you'll say is this —

BOLSHINTSOV In private?

DOCTOR In total privacy. 'Vera, I'm a man of few words — '

BOLSHINTSOV *silently repeats everything the* DOCTOR *says.*

' — but I have watched you for a long time. And I love you very much. And I want to marry you. And I want you to know that I love you best of all in maroon.'

BOLSHINTSOV Where's that?

DOCTOR 'Don't give me your answer now. I'll ask you again in a week's time — a month's time — a year's time.'

BOLSHINTSOV In a year's time I could be dead!

DOCTOR 'But I do love you very, very much and I know we could be very happy together.'

BOLSHINTSOV 'And I'm the greatest lecher in the whole province!'

DOCTOR Bolshintsov — !

BOLSHINTSOV Oh Christ! Here they are! (*Quietly, intensely*) And that was a rotten thing to say.

DOCTOR What was?

BOLSHINTSOV You're my doctor — you know my kidneys are perfect.

*Enter* NATALYA, MICHEL, VERA, ALEKSEY *and* LIZA-VETA. ALEKSEY *is carrying the kite and — as before — VERA holds the end of the tail.*

NATALYA Well, you two still here? You look very conspiratorial.

DOCTOR Babes in the wood, Natalya. You all know Bolshintsov, don't you? Aleksey Belyayev, the new tutor.

BOLSHINTSOV We've met. We've had a few chats. From what he tells me, we're a pair of dogs — aren't we?

DOCTOR And Vera you know.

BOLSHINTSOV Certainly do. And if she and I could have a moment of total privacy, I'd like —

DOCTOR So what's the big expedition?

NATALYA We're trying out Aleksey's new kite. Isn't it beautiful?

DOCTOR Indeed. What is it made of?

ALEKSEY Balsa wood. From tropical America.

NATALYA That's not the name you told me.

ALEKSEY Maybe I used the Latin name.

NATALYA Did you now. Trying to impress me?

VERA So tell us all the Latin name.

ALEKSEY  I will not.
   VERA  Because you don't know it.
ALEKSEY  *Ochroma Lagopus.*
   VERA  (*Laughs*) You made that up!
ALEKSEY  I'm warning you!
   VERA  He made that up just now!

*General talk and laugher during which:*

 DOCTOR  (*Privately to* LIZAVETA) I like your shoes.
LIZAVETA  Do you?
 DOCTOR  Very stylish.
LIZAVETA  They're French.
 DOCTOR  Beautiful.
NATALYA  (*Loudly*) This is an important event; so let's do it
         with proper formality. I'll lead off with the classical
         scholar. (*General laughter*) Vera, you and Mr
         Bolshintsov come next. Then Lizaveta and the
         Doctor. And Michel — you'll keep an eye on all of
         us, will you? Wait! Where's Kolya?
ALEKSEY  He's waiting for us down at the granary.
NATALYA  Right. Off we go.
BOLSHINTSOV  (*To* VERA) I haven't flown a kite for over fifty years,
         not since —
 DOCTOR  Move, Bolshintsov! You're holding up the column.
BOLSHINTSOV  Sorry.
 DOCTOR  What are you smiling at, Michel?
 MICHEL  At myself: tagging along at the rear.
 DOCTOR  The rear can easily become the front. All you need is
         a change of direction.
 MICHEL  I suppose I'll wait for that.
 DOCTOR  (*To* LIZAVETA) You must come out with me for a run
         in my new troika.
LIZAVETA  When did you get that?
 DOCTOR  Could arrive any of these days.
LIZAVETA  I'd love to, Doctor.
 DOCTOR  Excellent.

*End of Scene Two.*

# ACT ONE

## Scene Three

*The following day.*

*VERA is playing the piano offstage: John Field's midi No. 18 in E-major. The DOCTOR and MICHEL are sitting in the drawing-room. They have just had coffee.*

DOCTOR  Good coffee. Enjoyed that. The caffeine makes the brain gallop. And nobody makes coffee like the Kenyans. Or maybe you're a Brazilian, are you?

MICHEL  You wanted to talk to me, Doctor?

DOCTOR  Certainly did. Let me take this (*cup*) out of your way. Because of all my good friends you are the most perceptive, the most simpatico. At first I thought I'd go to Arkady and ask his help; but then Arkady isn't quite so astute in these matters as —

MICHEL  You want me to do something for you.

DOCTOR  Aha! No bluffing that razor intelligence! That's why I decided that if anybody could —

MICHEL  Doctor.

DOCTOR  To the point. (*Picks a crumb off MICHEL's knee*) Crumb on knee. Long story short. Bolshintsov has taken an enormous fancy to our young musician.

MICHEL  To Vera!

DOCTOR  Herself.

MICHEL  Bolshintsov!

DOCTOR  Himself.

*The music stops suddenly.*

MICHEL  Come on, man! Bolshintsov's a stupid old fool and she's only a child!

*Enter* KATYA *with fresh coffee. On her heels —*
*clearly following her and clearly distraught — comes*
MATVEY *carrying logs.*

DOCTOR  Inaccurate on both counts, Michel, if I may say so.
        She is not a child; and Bolshintsov is neither stupid,
        nor old, nor — (*Irritably to* KATYA) What is it, girl?

KATYA   Can I give you some coffee?

DOCTOR  None for me. Michel?

KATYA   It's freshly made.

MICHEL  I'm finished, thanks.

DOCTOR  Could we have a little privacy, please? (*To* MATVEY)
        Can't that be done later, Matvey? (*To* KATYA) And
        take this tray with you.

KATYA   Certainly, Doctor.

*She picks up the tray and leaves.*

MATVEY  (*As* KATYA *passes*) You've got to speak to me.

KATYA   I've got to do nothing.

MATVEY  You can't just ignore me!

KATYA   Just watch me.

*She sweeps off.* MATVEY *stumbles after her.*

DOCTOR  Anyhow my good friend Bolshintsov comes to me
        and asks me to speak to Natalya on his behalf. So I
        spoke to Natalya. Natalya said no. Then Natalya
        said yes. I report back to Bolshintsov. Bolshintsov
        is ecstatic! You saw him yesterday — scarcely
        coherent with excitement! So far, so good, I thought.
        Now move quickly, Doctor. Iron hot — you know?
        So this morning I go again to Natalya and suggest as
        delicately as I can that *now* might be the time for her
        to have a word in the ear of young Vera. And how
        am I received? In one of her sulks! Barely civil to me!
        Absolutely refuses to speak to Bolshintsov! And
        poor Bolshintsov! — He becomes more frantic by
        the hour! Don't judge him so harshly, Michel. He's
        reliable, he's rich, he's mad about her — that's a

possible basis for marriage, isn't it? And what prospects has Vera in a remote place like this?

MICHEL So?

DOCTOR So what I ask you to do is speak to Natalya on Bolshintsov's behalf. A word from you and that big generous heart of his would dance with joy.

MICHEL What's in this for you, Doctor?

DOCTOR (*Innocently*) What do you mean?

MICHEL You're not match-making for nothing.

DOCTOR Oh God, if I had only a fraction of that acumen! All right — cards on table. So that I can minister to the old and the sick in the outlying areas —

MICHEL Doctor!

DOCTOR Bolshintsov is to provide me with . . . new transportation.

MICHEL He's giving you a horse.

DOCTOR In a word.

MICHEL Two horses?

DOCTOR Three.

MICHEL Shpigelsky!

DOCTOR And a wagonette! (*Great burst of laughter*) I'm a rogue, amn't I? I'm not a doctor at all — I'm a quack! (*Voices off*) You'll speak to her for me, won't you?

MICHEL Yes — yes — yes — yes — yes!

DOCTOR Simpatico — mutual.

*Enter* NATALYA *and* SCHAAF. NATALYA *is flushed, agitated, fiery.*

SCHAAF I request four days — that is all. I will be returned before the end of the week.

NATALYA I have allowed you to go home every month for the past six months, Herr Schaaf. You are abusing that generosity.

SCHAAF But my mama is eighty-five year of age and she loses her strength more and more every day.

NATALYA Your mama has been losing her strength daily ever since you came here.

SCHAAF I am her only masculine child and she —

NATALYA If you go home now, Herr Schaaf, I suggest you take

all your belongings with you. I have nothing more
to say.

DOCTOR (*Quickly*) Arkady's winnowing-machine is the talk
of the countryside. Let's go and inspect it, Herr
Schaaf. (*He takes* SCHAAF *by the elbow*) See you later.

SCHAAF She is too cold heart.

DOCTOR It's life that's cold heart, my friend. Why don't I look
in on your mama one of these days?

*SCHAAF and the* DOCTOR *exit.* VERA *plays the piano
off: Nocturne No. 5 in B-flat major.*

NATALYA I can't stop Herr Schaaf from running home to his
mother and I can't get the doctor to leave. Next thing
he'll be seeing his patients here.

MICHEL He's out of favour today?

NATALYA Still trying to match Vera and Bolshintsov, is he?

MICHEL Yes.

NATALYA There's something in that for him. As for Bolshintsov
— he's a fool.

MICHEL Yesterday he was in favour, too.

NATALYA Today is not yesterday.

MICHEL For everybody except me.

NATALYA What's that supposed to — ? Oh God, I know — I
know — I know; and I'm sorry, Michel; I'm very
sorry; please forgive me. Yesterday I was disgrace-
ful. I ate the head of everybody yesterday. But I
should never snap at you. I really mustn't.

MICHEL Doesn't matter.

NATALYA Oh yes, it does matter. Because you are the core of
my life, Michel. There's nobody in the world I love
the way I love you. You believe that, don't you?

MICHEL If you tell me.

*He tries to put his arms around her but she evades him
— her train of thought is unbroken.*

NATALYA I snapped at Lizaveta, too; told her I didn't give a
damn about her taking snuff but for God's sake to
snuff openly. Did she think she was fooling any-

body, slipping into the toilet every hour and coming out with her nose red and her eyes watering?

MICHEL You never — !

NATALYA And poor Grandmother — do you know what I said to her? Oh my God! That she was such a damned domineering mother, no wonder Arkady is such a mess. And the poor woman, her mouth fell open. And she stared at me with such pained eyes. And she was so shocked, so hurt, so wounded, she was beyond tears. And I knew there was no apology I could make; that even if I caught her in my arms, as I wanted to, and said Sorry — sorry — sorry — sorry, that it would be no good, no good at all.

MICHEL I'm sure she —

NATALYA Maybe I'm going off my head, Michel.

MICHEL Natalya —

NATALYA Maybe I am. I don't mean insane. I mean a kind of temporary . . . derangement. That's possible, isn't it? Am I just slightly demented, Doctor Shpigelsky — not profoundly, not permanently — but today, here, now? Because do you know what I feel, Michel — today, here, now? I feel . . . unhinged.

MICHEL You are perfectly hinged.

NATALYA And dangerously irresponsible — giddy, heady, almost hysterical with irresponsibility. And do you know why I feel like that, Michel? — Michel my faithful watcher, observer, analyst. Of course you must know. Master Aleksey Belyayev, the gauche young graduate, the tutor of my son, he has taken possession of my head. Ridiculous, isn't it? I know it is. Ridiculous and at my age pathetic. And here I am telling all this to you, the last person in the world I'd want to hurt. Oh God, Michel, I am the real mess. What's to become of me?

MICHEL I am sorry for you.

NATALYA Can you help me, Michel? Please help me.

MICHEL I told you I thought something had happened, that you had changed. And then when I saw you in the meadow yesterday, when he was flying that damned kite, then I knew for sure.

NATALYA Knew what?

MICHEL I saw you transformed in that meadow yesterday, Natalya. You couldn't take your eyes off him. When he sang, you sang. When he laughed, you laughed even louder. You were so happy — so animated with happiness — that you glowed; your eyes, your skin, your body, your whole personality. And because you existed only for him, only because of him, you became extraordinarily beautiful, more beautiful than I have ever seen you.

NATALYA Yes, yes, yes, he's such an attractive, vital, vigorous young man, and in that meadow yesterday his wild, reckless youth was wonderful, irresistible —

MICHEL I think we shouldn't talk about this any —

NATALYA And that's what I responded to, that's what intoxicated me. But that will pass. I'll sober up. Of course I will, the moment I — Please, Michel, please don't turn away from me.

MICHEL One minute he takes possession of your head; the next he's a passing intoxication.

NATALYA That's all it is.

MICHEL He has intoxicated you or he has possessed you — which?

NATALYA Michel, that's —

MICHEL Does it matter? Who cares?

NATALYA I understand why you're hurt. Give me your hand. I do know why you're angry. But please —

MICHEL Angry? The lap-dog angry? The jaded, boring old attendant angry? No, I'm not angry with you! I pity you for God's sake! You are pitiful, Natalya!

*He regrets this immediately. She cries quietly. Pause.*

The doctor and Bolshintsov want an answer from you.

NATALYA What?

MICHEL I promised the doctor I would talk to you. He wants you to speak to Vera.

NATALYA Yes . . . all right . . .

MICHEL Will I send her to you? Will you speak to her now?

NATALYA   Whatever you think about me, please don't look so coldly at me —
MICHEL   Will you speak to Vera now, Natalya?
NATALYA   Yes . . . yes . . . (*As he leaves*) Michel!

*But he has gone. Now* SCHAAF *enters.*

SCHAAF   I think about what you say to me. I copulate over it. You are correct. I am in error. Mama I visit too often. So I do not go. I stay.

*He bows stiffly and goes off.* NATALYA *goes to the mirror, adjusts her hair, makes an effort to control her emotions.* VERA *enters.*

VERA   Michel said you wanted me. (*Looks closely at her*) Are you all right, Natalya?
NATALYA   I'm fine, thanks. Just a bit warm. Sit down here beside me. It's time you and I had a 'serious talk'.
VERA   What about? Is something wrong?
NATALYA   That last piece you played — what was it?
VERA   Nocturne in B-flat major.
NATALYA   Beautiful. You're really a very accomplished pianist — you know that, don't you?
VERA   What's the serious talk about?
NATALYA   'Life' — 'your future' — great issues like that. (*Laughs*) Look at that anxious face! (*Quick hug*) I just want to tell you — to remind you — that this will always be your home and that I will always love you as fully and as openly as if you were my very own daughter. But you know all that, don't you?
VERA   Thank you.
NATALYA   But we've got to be practical, too — haven't we? You're no longer a child. You're a young woman. And even though you are an orphan and have no private means, one of these days you're going to find yourself managing your own home. Now, how will that appeal to you?
VERA   My own home?
NATALYA   Yes! And maybe much sooner than you think. Some-

body has asked my permission to marry you, Vera.

> VERA *stares at her in shock; then suddenly covers her*
> *face with her hands and sobs.* NATALYA *puts her arms*
> *around her.*

NATALYA Here — here — here — here — here. What's all this,
for heaven's sake? What's there to cry about?

VERA I'm in your power.

NATALYA You're in my — ! Oh my goodness, will you listen to
this baby. There (*handkerchief*). Shhhhhh — easy,
my love. You are my only daughter, my only darling
daughter, and I won't let anyone, anywhere ever say
a cross word to her. All right?

VERA Yes.

NATALYA Come closer to me. Put your arm around me. That's
better. No, you're not my daughter; we're closer
than that. We're sisters. Does that sniff mean yes?
I'm your older sister that you love and tell all your
secrets to. And supposing she says to you one day,
'Vera, there's somebody who wants to marry you!'
what's the first thought that comes into your head?
That you're too young? That you never really
thought of getting married?

VERA I suppose so . . . yes.

NATALYA But supposing again — just supposing — the man is
a good man and a kind man and prepared to wait in
the hope that one day — then what would you say?

VERA Whatever you want, Natalya.

NATALYA Stop that! That's not how you speak to your older
sister! And it's not what I want, darling; it's what
you want. That's all that matters.

VERA Who is he, Natalya?

NATALYA Guess.

VERA I can't.

NATALYA Try.

VERA Have I met him?

NATALYA Yes.

VERA Where?

NATALYA Here.

VERA   In this house?

NATALYA   You saw him yesterday.

VERA   Yesterday?

NATALYA   He's not a boy. Who wants a boy? And there may
be more dashing men around. But then — it's
Bolshintsov.

VERA   Bolshintsov!

*NATALYA nods. Suddenly VERA bursts out laughing;
then NATALYA.*

You're joking me, Natalya!

NATALYA   I'm not.

VERA   You are — you are — you are!

*NATALYA shakes her head.*

Bolshintsov! Oh my God!

*NATALYA suddenly gets to her feet.*

NATALYA   That's it. Serious talk finished. Forget it. Had you
burst into tears, I would have thought, 'Perhaps . . .
maybe'. But the moment you laughed, poor old
Bolshintsov dropped dead!

*They both laugh again, NATALYA hugs VERA quickly.*

VERA   I'm awful, amn't I?

NATALYA   All you children — silly geese — you all want to
marry for love.

VERA   You married Arkady for love, didn't you?

NATALYA   (*Brief pause*) Of course. And all you children are
right. Poor old Bolshintsov — never even came
under starter's orders. And it is awful of us to laugh
at him because he is a kind man and a generous
man. But you're right: can you imagine tossing
about in bed at night, crazed by the thought of those
puffy cheeks?

VERA   Or the bald head!

NATALYA   Or the bulging stomach! Stop it — stop it! We're a
          pair of scamps! But supposing — I'm your sister
          again — just supposing he were young — reason-
          ably attractive — wanted to marry you — what
          would you say then?

VERA   How could I answer a question like that?

NATALYA   Because you can't imagine Bolshintsov young and
          reasonably attractive — ?

VERA   No, no —

NATALYA   Or because you're in love with someone else?

VERA   No, I'm not.

NATALYA   You don't love anybody?

VERA   Yes, oh yes. I love you, Natalya.

NATALYA   (*Quick hug*) And I love you. Who else?

VERA   Kolya. I'm dying about Kolya. And Anna. Even
          Lizaveta — with reservations.

NATALYA   Arkady?

VERA   No reservations. (*Arms wide to indicate a full scale of
          love*) That much. You're so lucky.

NATALYA   I know. And Michel?

VERA   That much, too. (*Slightly smaller*) Maybe that much.

NATALYA   The doctor?

VERA   Maybe — maybe — maybe; what about — (*Smaller
          still*)? He fancies Lizaveta — (*Arms wide again*) — did
          you know that?

NATALYA   And the new tutor?

VERA   Aleksey?

NATALYA   Aleksey.

VERA   Yes, I like Aleksey.

NATALYA   Show me.

VERA   I couldn't, Natalya. I —

NATALYA   (*Arms wide, then wider*) That much? That much?
          More?

VERA   Maybe.

NATALYA   More? That much?

VERA   (*Very embarrassed*) I couldn't — I just couldn't —

NATALYA   (*Arms wide apart*) That much, Vera? Yes, he is an
          attractive young man, isn't he? If he weren't so shy.

VERA   Aleksey shy!

NATALYA   Isn't he?

VERA He's certainly not shy! But he's probably afraid of you.

NATALYA Afraid of me?

VERA No, not afraid; not at ease with you — that's what he says. And that's natural enough: you're his employer.

NATALYA But he's . . . at ease with everybody else?

VERA With me he is. And he's such a clown! When we're together we laugh all the time.

NATALYA At what?

VERA At one another — at everything — at nothing. He says all he has to do is — (*She wiggles her little finger*) — and I fall apart. And so I do. You saw him yesterday in the meadow — leaping about and clowning and singing. That's what he's like most of the time. But wait until he's a full month here and he won't be a bit uneasy with you. I've told him that and he does pay attention to me — even though he calls me Baby Face.

NATALYA I didn't know you were so close.

VERA We're not really close, maybe more like —

NATALYA Oh you are. Oh yes you are.

VERA Do you think so? No, we're not. Well maybe a tiny little bit.

NATALYA Believe me — you are very close.

VERA Do you really think so, Natalya?

NATALYA *puts her arm around her again.*

NATALYA I think so. And you think so, too. And if your older sister were to say to you, 'You are in love with him, Vera, aren't you?' what would you say to her?

NATALYA *gazes into* VERA's *eyes for a long time.*

I know what you would say to her.

*She buries* VERA's *face in her breasts.*

You are in love, my darling.

VERA  Am I?

NATALYA  Yes, you are in love.

VERA  I don't know what's wrong with me.

NATALYA  Oh yes, you are, you poor, poor soul.

VERA  I don't know anything any more, Natalya.

NATALYA  And Aleksey — is he in love with you?

VERA  How could he be?

NATALYA  Because you are very beautiful. Because you are very, very young.

VERA  Two or three times he has caught my hand in his hands. And sometimes I have seen him looking strangely at me. But I can't read his eyes. I just don't know. And I wish to God I knew, Natalya. It's not knowing that —

*She breaks off because she sees the expression on* NATALYA's *face.*

What's the matter? You're very white. Are you all right, Natalya?

NATALYA  I'm fine — really — I'm —

VERA  I'll get Katya to bring you —

NATALYA  (*Very sharply*) You'll get nobody! (*In control again*) It's only the heat. Now, please, go back to your piano and play that nocturne again. Play it for me.

VERA  I have annoyed you — have I? You're angry with me because —

NATALYA  No, my dear; I'm not at all angry with you. Go back to your music.

VERA  Natalya, you know I love you and I wouldn't —

NATALYA  Love — love — love — you're so prodigal with that word, child. Leave me. Please. 'Bye.

VERA *leaves reluctantly.*

NATALYA  So now you know: they are in love!
Yes, they are in love.
Then God bless them.
Yes, God bless the fools.
You know you're jealous of her.

Jealous of a child?

Oh yes. And for the first time in your life you're in love yourself.

Don't be stupid!

Oh yes; you're in love with Aleksey.

He's afraid of me!

But you are in love with him.

Am I? Oh God, am I mad?

So what are you going to do about it?

He's got to leave. That's the only answer.

But supposing — just supposing — Vera has read it all wrong.

What does that mean?

You know she loves *him*. But you don't really know what he feels about her, do you?

So what?

So she may only imagine he's in love with her.

So — so — so — so — so?

So why not ask him straight it out: do you love Vera?

God, I couldn't, could I?

Why not? At this stage what pride have you left?

Very little. None.

Oh God — oh God — listen to yourself, Natalya. If you're not careful you're going to end up loathing yourself.

MICHEL *enters. He sits beside her.*

MICHEL  I want to apologise, Natalya. There's no excuse for the way I behaved. Please forgive me. When you have settled for very little and then you find that even that is slipping away, you're liable to . . .

*He realises she has not heard a word he has said.*

It's me, Natalya. The old lap-dog. Remember?

*She catches his hand.*

Am I forgiven?

NATALYA I have spoken to her, Michel. They're in love.

MICHEL (*Urgently*) And that's why you've got to extricate yourself, Natalya. Between them you'll be torn apart.

NATALYA I was prepared to marry her off to an old man, just to be rid of her. What's become of me, Michel?

MICHEL For the first time in years I see things clearly. And what has to be done is this: I am going to leave, Natalya — no, listen — please — just listen. For your sake, my love. Only for your sake. Aleksey must leave, too. I'll talk to him. I'll take him with me.

NATALYA Michel, I —

MICHEL For me to talk to you about duty — your home — Arkady — that would be a bit hollow, wouldn't it? But with Aleksey and myself out of your life, in time, in time this terrible disquiet will subside and your life will find an equilibrium again. And in time, my love, in time certain conciliations — recon- ciliations — all right, maybe they're only resigna- tions — but they will come about and you will find a measure of content, maybe of happiness, again. I promise you.

NATALYA So you're deserting me?

MICHEL No — never. What I'm advising —

NATALYA After you've lectured me on my duties and respon- sibilities. Wonderful, Michel!

MICHEL What I said was —

NATALYA For God's sake what's all the fuss about? Have we lost all sense of balance. The house is in turmoil because two stupid young fools are infatuated with one another? Good luck to them, I say. And to you, Michel, I say: Go, friend, go. You are a wonderful support.

MICHEL I am not walking out on you, Natalya. All right — Aleksey goes today — I'll talk to him now; and I'll stay with you until the end of the week, until you feel you're —

NATALYA (*In triumph*) Ah! A cunning lap-dog!

MICHEL Natalya —

NATALYA Aleksey goes but Michel stays! 'And in time, my

love, in time — '

MICHEL (*Angry*) For God's sake, woman!

NATALYA But let me tell you this: If you say a word to Aleksey, just one word, I'll never speak to you again!

MICHEL All right. But you'll tell him to go?

NATALYA Anything that has to be said to him I'll say it.

MICHEL So you'll tell him to go?

NATALYA That's my business.

MICHEL But you'll tell him to go?

NATALYA (*Shouts*) For God's sake!

MICHEL You're right, Natalya: I don't know what has become of you.

*He moves away.*

NATALYA Michel, Michel, don't go — please — for God's sake don't leave me.

*She rushes to him and embraces him desperately. Through her tears:*

My love — my love — my love — oh my love . . .

*Enter* ARKADY *and* ANNA, ALEKSEY *between them. He is showing Kolya's drawings in an exercise-book.*

ALEKSEY And he did that one last night — horses.

ARKADY They're wonderful horses. Look, Mother.

*But* ANNA *is staring at* MICHEL *and* NATALYA. ALEKSEY *and* ARKADY *now stare at them.* MICHEL *and* NATALYA *separate quickly.* ARKADY *is suddenly very quiet, very still, almost inaudible.*

ARKADY What — what's all this?

MICHEL It's not at all what you think, Arkady. Trust me.

*ARKADY stares at him for a few seconds. Then he moves towards NATALYA.*

ARKADY Natalya?

MICHEL As your friend, I —

ARKADY I need some explanation from you, Natalya.

ANNA Arkady —

ARKADY What have you to say to me?

ANNA We can all discuss this at some —

ARKADY I'm talking to you, Natalya.

*When she does not answer he turns to his mother.*

She won't speak to me.

ANNA She's upset and —

ARKADY Why won't my wife speak to me?

MICHEL It's all perfectly above board, Arkady. I promise you. I'll explain it all to you. I give you my word. We were discussing —

ARKADY (*To* ANNA) His word — he gives me his word.

MICHEL Arkady, believe me — trust me —

ARKADY (*To* ALEKSEY) You are showing me my son's drawings; we walk into this room; I find my wife and the man I believed was one of my closest friends —

MICHEL Arkady, trust me —

ARKADY (*Screams*) For Christ's sake don't use that word!

ARKADY *begins to sob.*

MICHEL I do know how distresed you must be —

ANNA I don't think you do, Sir. I don't think you have any idea at all — not now nor since you first came to this house.

*She takes* ARKADY's *arm and leads him off.*

I would like to know what passion is so magnificent it can justify this.

MICHEL *holds the door open.* ANNA *and* ARKADY *leave.* MICHEL *looks quickly, irresolutely at* NATALYA *— and exits too.* ALEKSEY *does not know what to do — Stay? Leave? He decides to go.*

NATALYA *(Icy, imperious)* Where are you going? *(He stops)* It's called a domestic scene. You've seen a few in your time, I'm sure, when your father came staggering home from his labouring job. *(Pause)* I don't have to explain myself to anyone — certainly not to you; but there is nothing between Michel and me. *(Pause)* Vera has told me about you two.

ALEKSEY Told you what? What is there to tell?

NATALYA Don't you know? *(She studies his face)* I really think the boy doesn't know.

*She smiles. The icy, imperious manner vanishes.*

Why are you so wary of me, Aleksey? Here — sit here beside me. I'll tell you what Vera told me: that she loves you.

ALEKSEY She said that to you!

NATALYA That she is in love with you.

ALEKSEY Oh, God, no. That's awful. God, poor Vera.

NATALYA Poor Vera indeed. But that's what she thinks. And what we must do — since we both love her dearly — we must protect her from as much hurt as possible. You do want to help, don't you?

ALEKSEY Yes, of course I do.

NATALYA Good. So; no more walks alone in the garden; no more of those silly, laughing games you play together — *(She wiggles her little finger)* — no more pranks on the swing.

ALEKSEY I can't change just like that. That would hurt her even more.

NATALYA Are you saying I've misread the whole situation?

ALEKSEY I don't know what you mean.

NATALYA You are in love with each other — is that it?

ALEKSEY No, we're not! No, I'm not! Whatever about her, I'm certainly not! I'll talk to her — tell her she's got it all wrong — as gently as I can. I'll do that just now. Then I'll pack my bag and leave.

NATALYA *(Furiously)* I'll make that decision! *(Calm)* What about your responsibility to Kolya, your duty to me?

ALEKSEY I'll get a substitute. I have a friend who —

NATALYA I'm sorry, Aleksey. If you want to go, then of course go.

ALEKSEY You know that's not what I want. You know very well how much I love it here.

NATALYA But we can't have you performing your duties under duress, can we?

ALEKSEY I'll stay.

NATALYA You'll go — you'll stay. Are you always so fickle?

ALEKSEY I'll stay. Yes, I'll stay as long as you want me to stay.

> *They look at each other for several seconds and then* NATALYA *turns away.*

NATALYA On the other hand perhaps you should go. Let's wait and see. Would you tell Michel I want him? He's probably in the study.

> ALEKSEY *moves off.*

One other thing, Aleksey.

> *He stops.*

Don't talk to Vera — not just yet. Leave her in her dream life for the moment.

> *Now he exits. And suddenly she is wildly triumphant — and uncertain.*

So now you know: he doesn't love her!
Yes — yes — yes.
Everything's falling into place!
Is it?
Oh, yes. Meshing — meshing.
And what are you going to say to Michel? To Arkady? To Anna? To Vera? To the world?
I don't give a damn!
You don't care?
Oh yes, I care. But not now — not now!

And him?
Yes him! Aleksey Belyayev, I love you!
But does he love you?
Time — time — give it time.
And he's staying?
Of course he's staying.
But he really should go.
Should he?
Oh yes — he really must go.
Why must he?
Because if he stays, Natalya . . . (*She hugs herself. Her face is alight*) . . . if he stays . . . you are lost.

*Music: Nocturne No. 5 in B-flat major.*
*Curtain. End of Act One.*

# ACT TWO

## Scene One

*Afternoon the following day. The garden as in Act One, Scene Two. Enter* SHPIGELSKY *and* LIZAVETA, *returning from a walk. He is peeling an orange.*

LIZAVETA  What have *you* heard?
DOCTOR  (*Indifferently*) Nothing.
LIZAVETA  You must have heard something?
DOCTOR  Not a word. Let's sit down.

*They sit in the gazebo.*

LIZAVETA  Well, whatever happened, the house is crazy today. The tutor has locked himself in his room — packing his bags, according to Nanny. Now, if she's right, the question is: Has Natalya sacked him or is he just walking out? And if she has sacked him, why has she sacked him?
DOCTOR  (*Indifferently*) Why?
LIZAVETA  Isn't that what we're all dying to know! Was he getting too amorous — or maybe not amorous enough for Natalya?
DOCTOR  Nasty.
LIZAVETA  Yes. Sorry. And Vera went for a walk after breakfast and hasn't been seen since. And the old lady's getting all her meals sent up to her room. And Arkady's been out fishing on the lake since before daybreak!
DOCTOR  So?
LIZAVETA  Without a fishing rod! I'm telling you — mad, mad, mad. According to Katya — (*Lowers her voice*) —

Katya says what happened was this. Yesterday afternoon the old lady and Aleksey and Arkady just happened to walk into the drawing-room — and there they were! — Natalya and Michel!

DOCTOR There they were what?

LIZAVETA What just! That's the question!

DOCTOR You suggest zey ver coupling?

LIZAVETA God forgive you, they were not!

DOCTOR He wouldn't be — not that he isn't thinking about it all the time.

LIZAVETA Ignaty!

DOCTOR Wouldn't put it past her, though.

LIZAVETA Now that's nasty.

DOCTOR Sorry. Orange?

LIZAVETA Thanks. All the same — Shhh!

> MATVEY *and* KATYA *enter. She is carrying a basket of flowers. He is exuberant and dances in front of her, blocking her way. She is very angry — or pretends to be.*

MATVEY I knock. The door opens. A sweet little lady with red cheeks and silver hair.

KATYA God, I really hate you.

MATVEY 'Katya's mother?' 'Yes.' 'I'm Matvey.' 'Ah, Matvey! Welcome, Matvey! Come in! Come in!'

KATYA I'll never speak to you again.

MATVEY 'Little Katya talks about you all the time. When are you two getting married?'

KATYA Look, I wouldn't marry you if —

MATVEY 'Come and have dinner with us next Sunday. We'll fix everything up then.'

KATYA I'll not be there.

MATVEY 'But I'm crippled with rheumatism, dear lady. And I have the wrong spiritual disposition. And what about the chasm between our ages?'

KATYA You bastard!

MATVEY 'Age? Can't I see you're a splendid, handsome, virile, intelligent man.'

KATYA You're a damned liar!

74

MATVEY 'No wonder little Katya's dying about you.'

KATYA She never said that!

MATVEY 'She never stops talking about you.'

KATYA Get out of my road, you sneaky old . . . pig!

*She rushes off. He follows laughing.*

LIZAVETA Well — well — well — well! What d'you make of that?

DOCTOR Cat and curiosity — remember?

LIZAVETA And the word about the house is that herself and Herr Schaaf are a pair. Now he's a real pig — Schaaf.

DOCTOR Matvey has the same idea as myself.

LIZAVETA What idea's that?

DOCTOR What you and I have been skirting around for the past hour and a half.

LIZAVETA (*Coyly*) What have we been skirting around, Ignaty?

DOCTOR If you're going to go all fluttery and simpering on me again, Lizaveta, there's no point in . . . All right. Plain speech. I'm sick of trying to run a bachelor house. You're sick of being a companion to the old bird. We're not getting any younger. Is there any good reason why we shouldn't go ahead with . . . things? All right, we don't know a great deal about one another. But maybe that's no harm. For example what do I know about you? Tidy appearance; cautious manner; good company to be with when you're not being coy; sharp at times — that tongue can be very bitter —

LIZAVETA Is this kind of analysis really — ?

DOCTOR But that's because you're a spinster. Damned inquisitive — that's another spinsterish thing. But practical, sensible, feet on ground. And you tell me you're a good cook?

LIZAVETA And what do I know about you?

DOCTOR If all you know about me is what they know about me, then you don't know me at all. 'A breath of fresh air' — 'comedian' — hah! They're civil to me because I relieve their boredom. But in their hearts they hate the peasant in me. And I clown for them because that masks how deeply I detest them. Oh, yes — detest them! Let me show you the Shpigelsky without the mask — well, a portion of him. Youngest of fourteen. Born in a mud hovel. Dirt. Cold. Misery. Hungry every day of my life. Somehow managed to scramble into an education of sorts and became what you see — a mediocre doctor with a large practice and scarcely any money.

LIZAVETA  Everyone says you're a good doctor.

DOCTOR  I'm not. And if you ever get ill, I'll get another doctor for you. What else is there? A moody man. Don't talk a lot. But not a jealous man. And I don't think I'm a mean man. And that's about it: biography — potted.

LIZAVETA  I think you're far too severe on yourself.

DOCTOR  Accurate. Because if you agree to marry me, you must know you're not marrying the laughing, fawning, ingratiating Shpigelsky. You're teaming up with the bitter, angry, cunning peasant.

LIZAVETA  I still think you're much too —

DOCTOR  And if you think you could make a life with him, well and good. What age are you?

LIZAVETA  Thirty.

DOCTOR  You're forty if you're a day.

LIZAVETA  Actually I'm thirty-six.

DOCTOR  I'll settle for that. And you should give up that snuff.

LIZAVETA  Snuff! I never — !

*He holds up an admonishing finger.*

An occasional pinch keeps the head clear. And you drink!

DOCTOR  Point. Snuff away.

LIZAVETA  *(Softening)* I'm going to give it up anyway.

DOCTOR  A damn good woman, Lizaveta. I like you a lot. But I don't like hanging about. Could I have your answer in — say — a month? Six months? Maybe even a year?

LIZAVETA  You'll have it tomorrow morning, Ignaty.

*He stares at her in amazement. Then a huge smile covers his face.*

DOCTOR Now that's the kind of woman I love! I'm not much good at romantic stuff but maybe this once . . .

*He takes her hand, bends over it and kisses it. As he does:*

I hope you're not off simpering again?

LIZAVETA I'm not. You are.

SCHAAF *and* ALEKSEY *enter.* SCHAAF *has* ALEKSEY *by the elbow.* ALEKSEY *looks around for* VERA.

SCHAAF Speak the word again, Aleksey: Eis, Sah-ne-Eis.

ALEKSEY Sahne-Eis.

SCHAAF Gut. And now I tell you how I compose it: from milk fat, from sugar, from gelatin — gelatin, yes?

ALEKSEY Yes.

SCHAAF Ja. So I mix them together and I freeze them and then I have Sahne-Eis — delicious ice-cream.

*Now he sees the* DOCTOR *and* LIZAVETA.

SCHAAF Ah! Herr Doctor! And Lizaveta!

DOCTOR Herr Schaaf.

SCHAAF *wags a roguish finger at the* DOCTOR *and* LIZAVETA.

SCHAAF So you make lust in the gazebo, Doctor, yes? Very gut. Nice hot day for it. And now you all return to go home with me to taste my — Aleksey?

ALEKSEY Sahne-Eis.

SCHAAF Excellent. My ice-cream. Made with my hand. Lizaveta?

LIZAVETA Lovely, thank you. I didn't know you were a chef, too.

SCHAAF Oh yes, I am great chef — I am great scholar — I am

77

great sportsman with bow and arrow. Did you know, Lizaveta, at university I am prize-winning lecher?

DOCTOR  Archer, Herr Schaaf.

SCHAAF  Archer — Danke. And now we go and eat my Sahne-Eis. Aleksey?

ALEKSEY  Go ahead. I'll join you in a few minutes.

SCHAAF  We eat it on the lawn — Eis im Freien. This is very nice on hot day, Doctor. After lust-making.

> He puts a confident arm around LIZAVETA — to her alarm — and leads her and the DOCTOR off.
>     ALEKSEY is alone. He looks around for VERA. After a few seconds she enters. Unlike the last time we saw her she is now very still, very controlled. But we have a sense, too, that a breakdown could easily occur.

VERA  Thank you for coming. I was afraid Katya mightn't have got the message to you.

ALEKSEY  Have you been crying?

VERA  Sunburn. I've been walking for hours, preparing a very important speech I was going to make to you. But now that I'm with you . . .

ALEKSEY  You're looking wonderful, Vera.

VERA  So you're leaving us, Master Tutor?

ALEKSEY  Natalya told you that?

VERA  Yes.

ALEKSEY  Maybe . . . we'll see . . . nothing's decided.

VERA  She says you want to go. Is she telling the truth?

ALEKSEY  Well, I thought that — you know — in the circumstances . . . It would be wiser, wouldn't it?

VERA  She told you about the talk she and I had?

ALEKSEY  Yes.

VERA  That I said I was in love with you?

ALEKSEY  Yes.

VERA  She's so treacherous. She trapped me into saying things I shouldn't have said. And now I've said it again, haven't I?

> She begins to cry quietly. He takes her hand in his.

*She withdraws it.*

No, no. I'm fine. Honestly.

ALEKSEY And I love you, too. I really do. D'you know what I'm going to do this winter? Take piano lessons! And this time next year we'll meet somewhere and play duets together and laugh like we —

VERA Please, Aleksey. I'm not Baby Face any more.

ALEKSEY Of course you're not. You're a very beautiful woman that I have a great, great affection for; that I esteem. Beautiful; and sensitive; and open. I've been here a month; and it's been the happiest month of my life because of you. And the last thing I would want is to see that beautiful, sensitive, open woman hurt in any way at all. That's why I must leave. You know I'm right. Yes, you have my love, Vera, really — whatever the affection of a penniless, jobless graduate is worth . . . .

VERA Esteem — affection — love; maybe you're right; maybe they are synonymous; maybe they should be. The fools, the loose-mouths talk only of 'love'. But maybe we should all settle for esteem — just a little esteem. Come on, Aleksey — don't look so anxious. I'm in a mess — a mess — a mess — of course I am. But a mess entirely of my own making. For the first time in my life I had an experience I thought was unique; and I thought everybody must recognise it and rejoice with me. (*Laughs*) A fool. A loose-mouth. No, you're not responsible, Aleksey; you're only a bystander. And for all her deviousness, not her mess either. Of course she betrayed me and I'm angry with her for that. But I'm more sorry for her than angry because she's so confused. She doesn't recognise the unique any more. Maybe she never did. And now I think she's quite . . . demented.

ALEKSEY Come on, Vera.

VERA You have demented her.

ALEKSEY I have — !

VERA Because she's in love with you.

ALEKSEY  For God's sake, Vera — !

VERA  And madly jealous of me because she thought you were interested in me. That's why one minute you have to go — the next you stay. That's why she's scheming with the doctor to pair me off with old Bolshintsov.

ALEKSEY  You're not serious!

NATALYA *enters and watches them.*

VERA  And it all seems quite reasonable to her — because she loves you. That's what love does: makes the unreasonable perfectly reasonable. How do you feel about her?

ALEKSEY  Natalya?

VERA  Do you love her, Aleksey?

ALEKSEY  What are you — !

VERA  I think you do.

ALEKSEY  If you think I'm going to be —

VERA  Yes, you do. I hope it's unique for you.

NATALYA, *smiling resolutely, now joins them.*

NATALYA  So there you are! I've been searching all over for you two. (*To* ALEKSEY) You are very disobedient, Aleksey Belyayev: you promised me — no more walks alone in the garden.

ALEKSEY  I just happened to —

VERA  Aleksey's here because I asked him to join me here.

NATALYA  Playing one of your silly laughing games, are you?

ALEKSEY  We've just been chatting.

NATALYA  I love this old gazebo. Arkady and I used to meet here long ago. It was red then. Your hair needs a wash, darling. I'll do it tonight.

VERA  (*Softly*) I always wash my own hair, Natalya.

NATALYA  I got a wonderful new shampoo from Paris: *Volatile* — good name, isn't it? Do you know what I was thinking this morning? If we put the two sides in ringlets, we could comb the front —

VERA  (*Shouts*) Stop it, Natalya! Stop it!

NATALYA Darling — ?

VERA For God's sake stop this game-playing! I'm no longer a child, Natalya — nor your ward that you can manipulate —

NATALYA Vera, my love —

VERA Nor your younger sister that you can kiss and worm secrets out of and then betray shamelessly. *I am a woman, Natalya, and I am going to be treated like a woman.*

NATALYA My darling, you're upset and —

VERA Yes, I am very upset. Aleksey says he is leaving because of me — and that's dishonest. Yes, I love him — you know I love him. But if he goes, it's because of you.

NATALYA Vera —

VERA Because you are in love with him. And that's why you betrayed me — because you thought I was a rival. But I'm not a rival, Natalya — I wish to God I were — but I'm not — I'm not . . . .

*She suddenly breaks down, looks at them for a second — and then dashes off.* ALEKSEY *moves to follow her.*

NATALYA Don't go, Aleksey. Please.

*He stops.*

Vera is right: I have behaved disgracefully. I'm ashamed of myself. And it *is* time to stop the game-playing and to muster whatever residue of decency I may still have. So — this is the last time I will see you. Or talk to you. I have made my mind up: you are leaving.

ALEKSEY I've already packed my —

NATALYA And she's right, too, about me: I am in love with you. Strange how I can say it so calmly, isn't it? — without embarrassment; almost disinterestedly; so simply, as if it had nothing to do with anguish and despair and pain and a kind of madness. I have been in love with you since the first day you came here. I suppose that was what the game-playing was all about: moving towards that possibility, that discovery, that acknowledgement; and then deviously, frantically trying to protect it. Why am I telling you all this? It's the last thing I should want you to know about me, that I'm calculating and treacherous and — look at me — yes, so ridiculous. No, no, please; you don't have to say anything. Just to have to listen to a declaration of love from a woman you have no interest in, that's difficult enough. Anyhow . . . that's all I have to say . . . . (*Brisk*) So. You've packed? Good. You'll leave after lunch. Matvey'll drive you to the town. I'll send you the balance of your salary. We won't meet again. There are going to be no goodbyes.

ALEKSEY  I'm not going.

NATALYA  You are —

ALEKSEY  I won't! I can't! Never in my life have I met a woman like you.

NATALYA  Aleksey —

ALEKSEY  So elegant, so poised, so beautiful —

NATALYA  Please, Aleksey —

ALEKSEY  You have no idea how — how magnificent, how exotic you are to someone like me.

NATALYA  For God's sake stop —

ALEKSEY  This house, this style, this grace, this ease, this refinement, this symmetry, this elegance — for a month I pretended that of course I wasn't impressed. But I was overwhelmed — I was in awe, Natalya — mute with awe. And at the centre of all this elegance and grace, there you were — the core, the essence, the very epicentre of it, holding it all in place, releasing, dispensing its wonders. And you noticed me and you spoke to me and you were kind to me — to me! — Aleksey Belyayev, a nobody in shabby clothes holding the delicate hand of this luminous creature.

NATALYA  You're leaving tomorrow, Aleksey.

ALEKSEY  Yes, yes, yes, Vera's so right, so wise! I *am* in love with you! And you are in love with me!

*He embraces her and swings her round.*

Oh my God, you are unique, Natalya! And I am
unique! We are both unique!

NATALYA  And you'll leave tomorrow?

*He kisses her and at the same time swings her round.*

You'll leave tomorrow?

ALEKSEY  Tomorrow.

*Again he kisses her and swings her round.*

NATALYA  Tomorrow?
ALEKSEY  Tomorrow.

*Again he kisses her and swings her round.*

NATALYA  Tomorrow?
ALEKSEY  Tomorrow.

*Again he kisses her and swings her round.* MICHEL
*enters.*

NATALYA  Tomorrow.
ALEKSEY  Tomorrow — tomorrow — tomorrow.

*Again he kisses her and swings her round.*

NATALYA  No, don't go, Aleksey — don't go — don't ever go.
Oh please God no.

ALEKSEY *now sees* MICHEL *watching them. He
freezes. Now* NATALYA, *seeing* ALEKSEY's *face, turns
and sees* MICHEL *too. A few seconds of silence. Then*
ALEKSEY *in acute embarrassment runs off.*

MICHEL  Thought you were here. Arkady's looking for you.
He's just behind me.
NATALYA  Well, here I am.

MICHEL So you've made your decision? The young tutor isn't being sent away?

NATALYA I'm not going to be cross-questioned, Michel.

MICHEL And he ran off in embarrassment! But then he's new at the game.

NATALYA (*Looking around*) I had a scarf —

MICHEL And he's bright; give him time; he'll learn to dissemble. Indeed he may be the very man to answer that anguished question of yours, 'What's to become of me?'

NATALYA Did you see a scarf — ?

MICHEL That's the trouble with baring your soul, isn't it? You regret it later. All that inflated language, the emotional palpitations, the heaving passions. I've done it so often myself — in my foolishness. It occurred to me a while ago that we regret most of the things we say and we regret even more all the things we don't say; so that our lives just dribble away in remorse. (*Suddenly regretting his bitterness*) Natalya, if I could —

*Voices off.* MICHEL *breaks off.*

NATALYA (*Urgently*) Have you spoken to Arkady?

MICHEL What about?

NATALYA When he saw us together in the drawing-room — you were to give him an explanation.

MICHEL Yes — no, no, not yet. Don't worry — I'll speak to him tonight. We've nothing to hide, have we?

*Enter* ARKADY *and the* DOCTOR.

ARKADY We thought we had lost you, my darling! We've been searching all —

*He stops when he sees* MICHEL. *He refuses to look at him for the rest of the scene.*

NATALYA Is there some mystery? Here I am.

MICHEL So you are . . . yes . . .

*Pause.*

DOCTOR  (*Quickly*) Just telling Arkady about this man who
        goes to the doctor —
ARKADY  This is very comical — most comical.
DOCTOR  'Doctor, Doctor, I think I'm a pair of curtains.'
        'Curtains? Pull yourself together, man!' (*He holds his
        head*) I know — I know — I know — I know.

        ARKADY *laughs excessively.*

ARKADY  Pull yourself together! Because he thinks he's a pair
        of curtains!
MICHEL  They're getting worse, Doctor.
ARKADY  I love them. I'm the best audience you could have.

        *Brief pause.*

DOCTOR  One more. This is the last. I promise. 'Doctor,
        Doctor, I'm in agony. There's a teacher in my eye.'
ARKADY  Sorry — missed that — a what?
DOCTOR  A teacher.
ARKADY  Ah. A teacher. Yes?
DOCTOR  'A teacher? That's not a teacher, you fool! That's a
        pupil.' (*He spreads his arms*) Shoot me, please —
        shoot me.

        *A moment's hesitation. Then* ARKADY *laughs exces-
        sively again.*

ARKADY  A pupil! In his eye! Do you get it? Good one, Doctor!
        Great one!

        *The laughter dies. Awkward silence.*

        (*To* NATALYA) Did I interrupt another discussion?
MICHEL  I was telling Natalya —
ARKADY  Or just a continuation of the first one? Because
        whatever it's about, it must be of — of — of univer-
        sal importance — that's all I can say.

DOCTOR A bit of medical advice for you all.

ARKADY Of universal importance at least.

DOCTOR Dr Schaaf has made ice-cream. I've eaten it before. Lethal. (*To* NATALYA) By the way you're having a visitor later, Natalya. Bolshintsov, I'm afraid.

NATALYA I don't want him near this house again.

DOCTOR He's very insistent. And I've said that —

ARKADY If Natalya doesn't want him, Doctor, then let him know he's not welcome here. Nothing more to be said. Now — dinner time! Let's all go and eat.

*He holds his arm out to* NATALYA. *She takes it. They move off.*

DOCTOR (*To* MICHEL) And we know what our fate is, don't we?

MICHEL Do we?

DOCTOR Oh yes — to bring up the rear.

MICHEL Fine.

DOCTOR Or another way of putting it, Michel: we're hangers-on.

MICHEL Let me tell you something, Doctor — something I regret I haven't said to you before.

DOCTOR And what is that?

MICHEL I am really sick of you.

*A huge peal of laughter from the* DOCTOR.

DOCTOR Good heavens, isn't that a remarkable coincidence! Because I'm really sick of myself!

*End of Scene.*

# ACT TWO

## Scene Two

*The drawing-room the following morning.*
    ANNA *is sewing.* ARKADY, *tense and agitated, tries to conceal his unease in activity. He consults a list and passes various documents to* MATVEY.

ARKADY  (*Quickly, sharply*) It doesn't make sense. I just don't understand it. Do you, Mother? Updating survey maps at this time of year — that's a job for winter! (*To* MATVEY) Has the land-stewart nothing better to do?

MATVEY  He says —

ARKADY  All right — all right — we'll indulge him. That's the wheat-fields (*map*). The birch forest. The paddock area. What else does he want? (*Consults list again*) The lakes. Where are the lakes? Here we are.

MATVEY  And the lower meadows.

ARKADY  The lower meadows.

MATVEY  The new dam.

ARKADY  Weir — weir — weir! Why is everyone so stupid. It's a weir — not a dam.

MATVEY  That's all he wants for the moment.

ARKADY  They must be returned to me before the end of the month, Matvey.

MATVEY  Yessir.

ARKADY  They are not to be left in the bailiff's quarters.

MATVEY  Absolutely not. Trust Matvey. Is it too early for tea?

ARKADY  Mother — tea?

ANNA  No, thanks.

ARKADY  In half-an-hour. That's everything, Matvey, thank you.

MATVEY *hesitates, then goes to* ARKADY *and whispers in his ear.*

ARKADY Can't hear you! Speak up!

*More whispering.*

What for?

*More whispering.*

What's so very important to you?

*More whispering.*

We'll see — we'll see — talk to me next week. (*As* MATVEY *departs*) And Matvey — tell Monsieur Rakitin I'd like a word with him. He's in the billiard-room.

MATVEY *exits.*

ARKADY Such a strange request. Matvey wants three days off. Never had a day off in his life and now he wants three.

ANNA What for?

ARKADY Something about a wedding, I think. Three full days! He wouldn't know what to do with himself.

ANNA Let him have them, Arkady.

ARKADY I said I'll see; and I will.

ANNA Did I hear you walking about during the night?

ARKADY Did I waken you?

ANNA No, I was reading.

ARKADY Yes, the old mind was thrashing about a bit. So I moved into the nursery. Didn't want to disturb Natalya.

ANNA *puts away her sewing.*

ANNA Michel and you haven't spoken yet?

ARKADY (*Alert*) Sorry?

ANNA Michel hasn't offered you an . . . explanation yet, has he?

ARKADY That's why I've sent for him.

ANNA Ah.

ARKADY Since he hasn't volunteered to give me one, now I'm going to demand one. I *am* owed an explanation, Mother.

ANNA Of course.

ARKADY And if one isn't offered now, this very morning, then I'll insist on one.

ANNA There may well be a very simple explanation, Arkady; so simple we just can't see it.

ARKADY I'm prepared to listen. I'm not an unreasonable man. But this is my home, Mother; and I am head of this household; and I will not be treated casually by anybody under this roof — not by anybody.

ANNA Of course not.

ARKADY I mean to say — I walk into this room; and there is my wife with this man; and she is sobbing; and all he can say is, 'Trust me. Trust me.' I mean to say, even with the best will in the world, Mother, an explanation *is* necessary.

*She looks closely at him. He is on the point of tears. She goes to him.*

ANNA You work too hard. You're getting more like your father.

ARKADY Am I?

ANNA It's a pity you never knew him.

ARKADY I have a vague memory of him.

ANNA He was such a handsome man; and so talented; and so gracious; and so endlessly kind. I loved him very much. Yes; without reservation. And he doted on you. He would have been so proud to have seen you grown up and managing the estate so well — this estate that he fashioned out of a wilderness — gave his entire life to, really . . . . And all the years we were married, at the beginning of every month — you wouldn't remember; you were too young — he went to Moscow for three nights; to sell timber or grain; or to buy new horses or equipment. And to visit a lady there that he loved. Her name was Maria, I think. I never saw her but I was told she wasn't at all beautiful. Strange, wasn't it — and he was so ... so magnificent .... Every month for almost fifteen years. And throughout all those years he never mentioned her to me and I never mentioned her to him. Because he loved me, too. I know he did. And I loved him very much. Yes; without reservation. So what would there have been to say . . . except wounding things .... And he would have been so proud of little Kolya.

MICHEL *enters carrying a billiard cue.*

I'm glad that billiard table's being used again.

MICHEL It's a great table.

ANNA So my husband used to say. But if it weren't for you, Michel, it would be mildewed. You must play more often.

*She leaves.* MICHEL *is on the defensive. He looks at* ARKADY. ARKADY *is suddenly embarrassed and pretends to tidy his papers.*

MICHEL Matvey said you wanted me. (*Pause*) Do you want to see me, Arkady?

ARKADY You owe me something.

MICHEL Do I?

ARKADY You owe me an explanation.

MICHEL I don't think —

ARKADY I am owed an explanation. You promised me an explanation.

MICHEL What I said was —

ARKADY What you said was trust me; that's what you said; trust me; I can explain all this; there is a perfectly simple explanation, you said.

MICHEL And there is.

ARKADY   And that's what I want to hear — that perfectly
         simple explanation. I walk in here with my mother
         and that tutor fellow; and there are you and my
         wife. And can you imagine — have you any idea at
         all? — what I felt? — how I felt? — and my mother
         standing beside me? And then yesterday evening at
         the gazebo — there you are again — for a second
         time — for God's sake for a second time! — and, that
         charlatan Shpigelsky watching and listening and
         privately sneering and —

         *He breaks down. After he recovers:*

         I can't talk to you like this, Michel — we've known
         each other since we were boys — how can I talk to
         you like this? Oh my God, have you any idea how
         destroyed I am?
MICHEL   Arkady, I —
ARKADY   Just answer one question — please, please, just
         one question, please. I really don't want an explana-
         tion. For God's sake what good is an explanation?
         Just one question, Michel; and please answer it
         honestly. Are you in love with Natalya?
MICHEL   Yes.
ARKADY   So. There you are. Knew it. So there you are. Knew
         it for a long time of course. Oh yes. And I don't
         blame you — blame? — it's not a question of blame
         for God's sake. No, no; it's — it's understandable;
         that's what it is; quite understandable; she's such a
         beautiful woman that naturally men find her attrac-
         tive; and naturally, of course naturally, naturally —
         she responds to those attentions. And the trouble is
         — part of the trouble is — that you and she have so
         much more in common than she and I have — oh
         yes, yes, yes, you have. You're both so intelligent
         and so well-read and so sophisticated. Not that she
         doesn't love me — I'm not saying that — I know she
         loves me. But she responds to something in you I
         haven't got, can't give her. And I think I could have
         carried on — yes, I know I could — as long as she

was, you know — reasonably discreet. But those two occasions, here and at the gazebo — I mean I don't think — I really don't think I should have been subjected to that, Michel. But at the same time it would be wrong of me to deny her her freedom; I won't do that either; I can't crush another person's life. So what we must do, Michel — and Natalya, too — we must try to — to — to find some way of conducting our lives together — the three of us — as best we can — with discretion — without too much hurt — as best we can — however we can . . . . That's what we must do . . . please . . . .

*Pause.*

MICHEL   I know what we must do, Arkady. I must leave here.
ARKADY   Go away?
MICHEL   It's the only answer.
ARKADY   (*In panic*) Oh, God, no, Michel! Please!
MICHEL   By myself, Arkady. Alone.
ARKADY   Not with Natalya?
MICHEL   Not with Natalya. Alone.
ARKADY   But you love her —
MICHEL   I'll leave tomorrow. You know I'm right.
ARKADY   How will we tell Natalya? Oh God, better you tell her. No, I will. It's my duty. I will.

*Impetuously he flings his arms around* MICHEL.

God bless you, Michel. You are a very, very good man. Thank you. I said I couldn't deny her her freedom — and I couldn't — how could I? But if I let her go altogether, Michel, I don't think I would survive.
MICHEL   We all survive, Arkady.
ARKADY   Do we? Yes, I suppose we do. Even if we love without reservation.
MICHEL   Especially if we love without reservation.

ARKADY *embraces him briefly again.*

ARKADY  May God bless you abundantly.

> ALEKSEY *enters.*

ALEKSEY  Sorry. Am I — ?
ARKADY  Come ahead, Ivan — come on.
MICHEL  (*Whispers*) Aleksey.
ARKADY  Sorry — Aleksey. How can we help you?
ALEKSEY  This is a list of French books Kolya will need next term.
ARKADY  Good — splendid. Thank you. Just leave it there. And now, if you'll excuse me —

> *He is about to leave, turns, embraces* MICHEL *quickly again.*

The astonishing winnowing-machine is reluctant to winnow. Maybe that's what makes it astonishing!

> *He laughs heartily, nervously, and leaves.* MICHEL *goes over to the bookshelf and begins picking out his own books. His manner is brittle and edged with panic.*

MICHEL  I'm going to the town tomorrow. Can I give you a lift?
ALEKSEY  No, thanks.
MICHEL  *Tristram Shandy* — that's my copy. (*Removes the bookmark we saw in Act One, Scene One*) Never seem to get past page 115. Have you ever read it?
ALEKSEY  You're going shopping?
MICHEL  Leaving.
ALEKSEY  Leaving for good?
MICHEL  Business in Moscow. I was sure I had some Dickens here.
ALEKSEY  I thought you'd be here until —
MICHEL  Between these and the books upstairs I'll have to get an extra trunk.
ALEKSEY  Does Natalya know you're leaving?
MICHEL  Not yet. She'll be told.

*He goes to* ALEKSEY *and speaks directly into his face.*

All right, I'll tell you why I'm leaving, Aleksey. Arkady believes I'm in love with Natalya. Asked me straight out. And because he believes that, I have to leave, haven't I?

ALEKSEY Oh God.

MICHEL You'd do the same if you were in my position, wouldn't you?

ALEKSEY Oh my God.

MICHEL I imagine you're a big believer in 'love'. Am I right?

ALEKSEY Oh I — I —

MICHEL Yes you are.

ALEKSEY I've very little —

MICHEL Go on — admit it.

ALEKSEY I believe — I *think* — that if you love a woman and if she loves you — that must be a great happiness, mustn't it?

MICHEL Got it wrong, Aleksey, I'm afraid. All love is a catastrophe. Look at me. An endless process of shame and desolation and despair when you are stripped — you strip yourself! — of every semblance of dignity and self-respect; when you grovel in the hope of a casual word or a sly smile or a secret squeeze of the hand. But of course you think: that won't be my experience; poor old Rakitin — all his life he's been a hanger-on, the second man, made for humiliation, invites it with his 'loyalty', his subservience, doesn't he?

ALEKSEY Honest to God, Michel, I never thought of —

MICHEL Let me tell you just one thing. When you find yourself enslaved by love, owned by a woman, then for the first time in your life you will know what real suffering is. Yes; look at me.

*He gives a quick dry laugh. Pause.*

ALEKSEY I'm very sorry you're leaving, Michel.

MICHEL Thank you. Look after yourself.

ALEKSEY We'll all miss you.

MICHEL  For a day.

ALEKSEY  Well, I'll miss you. And I really am sorry you've been so . . . hurt.

> MICHEL, *embarrassed, quickly ruffles* ALEKSEY's *hair. And then quickly, spontaneously, the two men embrace. As they do,* NATALYA *enters, carrying a box of chocolates. She is alerted by the display of affection between the two men. She looks quickly from one to the other.*

NATALYA  Do you know where I've been for the past half-hour? Sitting under the lime tree in the walled garden, gorging myself on these. They're wonderful. (*To* ALEKSEY) Have one.

ALEKSEY  Thanks.

NATALYA  Have two. Have three. The perfume from that lime tree is so subtle.

> MICHEL *has returned to his books. She picks up the* Tristram Shandy.

NATALYA  We are never going to get through this *Tristram Shandy*, Michel. So what we've got to do is take ourselves in hand. You'll be a real sweetheart and every night after dinner you'll read me a full chapter — beginning tonight.

MICHEL  I'm leaving today, Natalya. In fact — now.

> *She looks quickly at* ALEKSEY *who is suddenly engrossed in Kolya's list.*

NATALYA  What do you mean?

MICHEL  Going to Moscow. Business.

NATALYA  But you'll be back?

MICHEL  We'll see. Perhaps. I'll make you a present of the Sterne. Maybe Aleksey'll read it to you.

NATALYA  You're not going now — just like that!

MICHEL  After I've finished packing. Then I'll say my good-byes.

MICHEL *exits. She tries to conceal her alarm — she laughs.*

NATALYA  Typical Michel. Totally unpredictable. God alone knows what goes on in that strange head of his. Now. Give me your hand. I want to tell you my plans. (*She takes* ALEKSEY's *hand*) This afternoon I'm going to visit my old nanny at a village called Spasskoye. It's about fifteen miles from here. And you are going to drive me. And we are going to have a picnic together on the bank of the —

*He suddenly winces and withdraws his hand.*

Oh I'm sorry. Did I hurt you?
ALEKSEY  No, I'm fine.
NATALYA  Don't know my own strength. Are you sure?
ALEKSEY  Fine — fine — really.
NATALYA  So that's agreed? Good. Can you swim?
ALEKSEY  Just about.
NATALYA  I'm sure you're a wonderful swimmer. And there's a lovely sandy beach there. And it's a perfect day for a drive.
ALEKSEY  If you'll excuse me, Natalya. I promised Michel I'd help him to pack.
ARKADY  (*Off, calling*) Aleksey! Where are you?
ALEKSEY  (*Calling*) In the drawing-room.
NATALYA  So that's agreed?

ARKADY *enters.*

ARKADY  We need help out here. (*To* NATALYA) Oh, I love that dress! You look astonishing in that dress! (*To* ALEKSEY) The winnowing-machine's stuck in the mud. Come on, boy. We need your muscle.

ARKADY *exits.*

NATALYA  That's agreed, Aleksey?
ALEKSEY  Yes — yes —

*The* DOCTOR *and* VERA *enter.*

NATALYA (*Anxiously*) And we'll leave about three?
ALEKSEY Fine — yes — yes — fine. (*To* VERA) I'm not running away. I'm needed. I'll be straight back.

ALEKSEY *exits.*

DOCTOR Have you heard the news, Natalya? Michel's leaving!
NATALYA Yes.
DOCTOR Today! Now!
NATALYA I know.
DOCTOR Good Lord! Business in Moscow, he says. Well — well — well — well. And what's the commotion in the yard?
NATALYA The damn winnowing-machine — it's stuck again, I think.
DOCTOR That's the way with those machines: some you winnow, some you lose-ow. (*He holds his head as before*) Sorry — sorry — sorry — sorry.
VERA Aren't we going to get tea this morning?
DOCTOR Indeed. Good idea.

*He goes to the door and calls.*

Matvey! Where are you?

NATALYA *speaks softly and intimately to* VERA *who remains icy throughout.*

NATALYA I'll say it once more and never again. What I did was wrong. I can't explain why I did it. But it's done. And I'm sorry. And I apologise.
VERA (*To* DOCTOR) If he's in the kitchen he won't hear you.
DOCTOR (*Louder*) Matvey!
NATALYA And you've got to stop this childish sulking.
VERA Why are you so agitated? He does love you. Hasn't he told you yet?
NATALYA I'm sending him away.
VERA (*Mirthless laugh*) He goes — he stays — he goes — he

97

stays. You're very unsure of him, aren't you? And what if you lost him now after all that duplicity?

NATALYA  You're a vicious little vixen, aren't you!

*NATALYA leaves. The DOCTOR goes to VERA.*

DOCTOR  Either he doesn't hear me or he's ignoring me.

*He now sees that NATALYA is gone. He looks intently into VERA's face.*

Do you want to tell me why you're so sad?

*She shrugs. He goes through his pantomime of taking her pulse.*

Far too fast. Is the heart a bit . . . perturbed? (*Wearily and in self-mockery*) A man came up to me this morning. 'Help me, Doctor. I'm Aikin from Neuralgia.' 'Glad to meet you. I'm Shpigelsky from Gorlovka.' (*Pause*) If the mask fits, wear it, I say.

VERA  Tell me about Bolshintsov, Doctor.

DOCTOR  (*Eagerly*) Happily! What do you want to know? Ask me anything about him — anything at all.

VERA  I've really only one question.

DOCTOR  Very, *very* well off — I promise you. Owns the biggest farm from here to —

*He breaks off because KATYA enters. She is smiling serenely.*

(*Irritably*) Well — well — what is it, girl?

KATYA  You called, Doctor.

DOCTOR  What for?

KATYA  I can't read minds, Doctor, can I?

DOCTOR  What are you talking about?

KATYA  You called for Matvey. I am here in Matvey's place.

DOCTOR  Yes — tea — tell him to serve tea in here.

KATYA  Matvey is engaged elsewhere, Doctor. But his responsibilities are now my responsibilities and I am very happy to share them with him.

DOCTOR (*To* VERA) What's the girl ranting about?

KATYA Tea for two? For three? For everybody?

DOCTOR If I'm not disrupting your life too much.

KATYA Not at all, Doctor. It is my pleasure. And Matvey's.

*She exits.*

DOCTOR Good God! Touch of sunstroke, maybe. Anyhow —
Bolshintsov. Wealthy. Gentlemanly. Considerate.
Quite sophisticated — in a rural sort of way. What's
your one question?

VERA If I displeased him, is he the kind of man who would
strike me?

*The* DOCTOR *stares at her in amazement. Then he
takes her in his arms as if she were a child and rocks
her.*

DOCTOR Never — never — never — never — oh never. Oh
my sweet, sad-eyed child, what can I say to you?
He's old; and fat; and stupid; so stupid he thinks
my jokes are funny. And yes, he's quite well off.
And he seems to like you. And he's kind enough, I
suppose. What more can I tell you, little one? If I
thought for a moment that love was a necessary —
even a desirable — ingredient in these matters, then
I'd say: pass this up. But since I don't . . . (*He shrugs*)
He's bird in hand, I suppose . . . .

*Pause.*

VERA (*Quickly, resolutely*) I'll marry him, Doctor.

DOCTOR You'll wait until —

VERA I said I'll marry him. Tell him I'll marry him.

DOCTOR Vera, you'll —

VERA But I won't wait. It has to be now — as soon as
possible. Will you tell him that?

*He spreads his hands and nods his head.* SCHAAF

*enters rapidly, barely hesitating as he dashes through the room.*

SCHAAF You hear the tidings? Michel is exiting — even now as we prattle. (*He takes the* DOCTOR *by the elbow*) Come. We tell him goodbye. Then I go riding. You go riding with me, Doctor?

DOCTOR Sorry, Herr Schaaf. Calls all afternoon.

SCHAAF (*To* ALEKSEY *who enters*) We tell goodbye to Michel. He exits even now as we prattle.

*They both leave.*

ALEKSEY I'm glad you're alone.

VERA (*Embarrassed*) I thought you were helping with the — ?

ALEKSEY I was. Then I helped Michel pack. Then I packed my own things.

VERA Why? Are you — ?

ALEKSEY I've got to leave, Vera. Today. Now. You know I have. I had a strange talk with Michel a while ago; and looking at him, listening to him, suddenly there were no more confusions: Get out! — get out! — get out! Do I sound sort of frantic? I suppose I am. Part of my mind is hysterical but part of it is wonderfully lucid. I'm here a month and what happens? Arkady fights with Michel. Michel fights with Natalya. Natalya fights with you. Anna fights with Michel. And in some way I seem to be the cause of it all. And now Michel is leaving. And I'm leaving.

VERA And I'm leaving.

ALEKSEY (*Not listening to her*) Good for you. I'm so far out of my depth, Vera, I can scarcely breathe. Of course they're kind and thoughtful and intelligent people. But honest to God I never want to see any of them ever again.

VERA But you love her, Aleksey.

ALEKSEY That's exactly what I'm saying: that was part of the hysteria, the madness. A Chinese squib — a quick, blinding flash — then nothing.

VERA Nothing?

100

*He catches her hand.*

ALEKSEY But it was a good month, too, Vera, thanks to you. A great month. All those laughs — Nanny coming off the swing? — hiding Matvey's wellington in the oven? — remember? — putting pepper in Lizaveta's snuff-box? Terrible to think we'll have forgotten it all by Christmas.

*He kisses her casually on the top of the head.*

ALEKSEY I'm serious about those piano lessons though. Right?
VERA Right.
ALEKSEY I'm leaving now — on foot. Michel's going to pick me up somewhere along the road. (*As he goes*) Be good.

*He goes quickly to the door — stops — returns to* VERA.

God, the head's really gone. I can't face Natalya. Give her that (*note*), would you? Read it if you like. 'Goodbye' — that's all it says.

*He runs off. He almost bumps into* SCHAAF *in the doorway. As before* SCHAAF *is rushing. He holds a pair of riding-boots in his hand.*

'Bye, Herr Schaaf.

ALEKSEY *exits.*

SCHAAF "Bye?' But I am not going nowhere. "Bye?' Why does he confuse me? And Katya she hides on me. She was to have polish my boots but she did not. And now she hides.
VERA Did you try the clothes line?
SCHAAF No, no; I look there. She hides on me today. Why is that?

NATALYA *enters.*

You know where Katya is?

NATALYA No idea.

SCHAAF I try her bedroom — laundry — clothes line — kitchen — her bedroom again — no Katya. And look (*boots*) — still soiled.

*He goes off.* NATALYA *puts away her painting things. As she does:*

NATALYA I'll be away all afternoon, Vera. Nanny'll look after Kolya but I'd be glad if you gave a hand.

VERA Of course. (*She holds out the note*) For you.

NATALYA You haven't anything else to do, have you?

VERA Nothing.

NATALYA *holds out her hand to take the note — and knows instinctively what is in it.*

NATALYA Aleksey?

VERA Yes.

NATALYA He's going?

VERA Yes.

NATALYA He's already gone?

VERA I think so.

NATALYA Oh my God . . . (*Opens note*) 'Goodbye'. The eloquent Aleksey Belyayev . . .

*She is about to cry. Then with a burst of sudden passion:*

How dare he, the pup! The jumped-up, baby-faced pup! Who the hell does he think he is! Well he's not walking away like that! I'm not one of his college sluts! He'll go *if* I say he goes! He'll go *when* I say he goes! And who is he to decide I haven't the courage to throw all this up and go with him! If that decision is to be made, it'll be my decision — not his! The bastard! (*About to break down*) Oh my God . . .

VERA   It's better he's gone. You know that.

NATALYA   Everything's in such a mess . . . . I'm afraid I can't hold on much longer . . . .

VERA   Everything'll soon be back to normal.

NATALYA   For God's sake can't you see it's the normal that's deranging me, child?

ARKADY *enters.*

VERA   I'm leaving, too.

NATALYA   The sooner the better. I wish you were all gone. I can't tell you how sick I am of all of you.

ARKADY   (*Privately to* VERA) How does she know he's going?

VERA   (*Puzzled*) He left a note for her.

ARKADY   Damn it, we agreed I'd tell her. That was my duty.

*He goes to* NATALYA *and puts his arm around her.*

It's all right, my darling. Everything's in hand. Michel and I had a wonderfully open talk. I don't want an explanation. I don't need an explanation. All I need is you. (*He lifts her head and looks into her face*) Do you hear me, my darling? You are all I need.

*Enter* KATYA *with a tray.*

(*Sharply*) Not now, girl.

KATYA *takes in the scene and exits.*

Let me tell you what we'll do. You'll lie down for an hour and I'll bring you up a cup of hot chocolate — remember the famous hot chocolate I used to make for you when you were expecting Kolya? And in no time at all you'll be a new woman — a new and even more beautiful woman — in no time at all.

NATALYA   Yes. I'll go to my room. (*Removing his supporting hand*) No, please, Arkady. I can manage.

*She picks up her paints and is about to leave when* MICHEL *enters.*

MICHEL I came to say goodbye.

ARKADY (*Privately*) We agreed I'd tell her, Michel. Now look at the state she's in.

MICHEL I don't think I'm the cause this time, Arkady.

ARKADY Then who — ?

MICHEL Goodbye, Natalya.

*No answer.*

ARKADY Michel's leaving, my love.

*Pause.* ARKADY *puts his arm round* MICHEL'*s shoulder and hugs him.*

But he'll be back. I'm insisting on that. We can't afford to lose a good friend like Michel. Amn't I right?

NATALYA *is about to speak, is overcome with tears — and dashes off.* VERA *follows her.*

VERA She'll be fine. Don't worry.

VERA *exits.* ARKADY *tries to cover his embarrassment with bluster.*

ARKADY And I mean that, Michel. You know that. Come and spend Christmas with us! Please. I'd love you to. She would, too. I know she would — We both know she would.

MICHEL Thank you.

ARKADY No, no, my friend; I thank you. What you are doing is . . . noble!

*And again he embraces* MICHEL. *Suddenly the door opens and in come* LIZAVETA, ANNA, SCHAAF *and the* DOCTOR. *Everybody speaks at the same time.*

DOCTOR   Well — where is she?

ARKADY   What? Who?

DOCTOR   Katya said she was ill.

LIZAVETA   Did she faint?

MICHEL   If you'll excuse me —

ANNA   Natalya, Arkady.

ARKADY   Ah. She's gone to her room — to lie down.

LIZAVETA   (To DOCTOR) Go and have a look at her.

MICHEL   Goodbye, Herr Schaaf.

SCHAAF   "Bye? — ''Bye?' — But I am not going nowhere!

DOCTOR   She's in her room now?

LIZAVETA   Is Vera with her?

ARKADY   Perhaps leave her for a while.

ANNA   Was it some sort of weak turn?

ARKADY   I promise you — she's fine.

MICHEL   I'm about to leave, everybody.

ANNA   That little Katya exaggerates.

LIZAVETA   If I can be of any help?

SCHAAF   All day people tell me 'Bye — 'Bye — 'Bye.

ARKADY   Goodbye, Herr Schaaf.

SCHAAF   But I am not exiting!

ARKADY   Ah. Splendid.

ANNA   That little maid's been behaving strangely all day.

MICHEL   I'm afraid I have to go —

ARKADY *holds his hand up for silence.*

ARKADY   Please — please — please — please — please.

DOCTOR   Tell me this: How much of that ice-cream did she have?

SCHAAF   Why do you ask about my — ?

ARKADY   Please! Natalya is perfectly well — wonderfully well. Thank you all for your concern. But I promise you there is nothing, nothing at all to worry about. Now. I need help with the accounts. Where's Ivan?

ANNA   The blacksmith is illiterate, Arkady — you know that.

ARKADY   Of course I know the blacksmith is illiterate. I'm talking about Ivan the —

MICHEL   He means Aleksey, the tutor.

ARKADY  Aleksey! Why do I always get that wrong!
MICHEL  Aleksey has just left.

> *This is greeted with general surprise: What? When did this happen? Why did he go? Did he say goodbye to you? Does Kolya know?*

SCHAAF  He go also? Mein Gott. Everybody is 'Bye — 'Bye — 'Bye.
ARKADY  (*Privately*) When did this happen? He's in my employment! How can he walk out without — ?
MICHEL  Shhh. Vera fell in love with him.
ARKADY  Our little — ? With the tutor?
MICHEL  And I'm afraid he didn't love her. So the kindest thing he could do was . . .
ARKADY  Leave?

> MICHEL *nods.*

Good heavens! Everybody's leaving! Everybody's being so noble! The world is suddenly becoming a wonderful place, Michel! (*To* ANNA *who has joined them*) But now we have another problem, Mother: Who will teach Kolya his French and English?
SCHAAF  (*Overhearing*) I will pedagogue him, Arkady. I am happy. Especially in English.
ARKADY  Most kind of you, Herr Schaaf. That's a splendid suggestion . . . I'm sure . . . .

> ANNA *and* MICHEL *find themselves together.*

ANNA  This house will suddenly be very quiet.
MICHEL  This house is never quiet.
ANNA  With you and the young tutor gone? Oh, yes. Natalya'll especially miss you both.
MICHEL  Maybe.
ANNA  Strange, isn't it? She has the unqualified love of a very good man. But for some women — and for many men — that doesn't seem to be enough. And instead of that love satisfying, enriching, it becomes

another form of . . . suffocation. So that all of their life is dissatisfying, even turbulent. And the people who offer their love without reservation, even though that love is neither fully appreciated nor fully reciprocated, they are the fortunate ones . . . strange as it may seem . . . even though they don't believe they are . . . . I hope you have a very good journey, Michel. And I hope you will come back to us very soon.

*The DOCTOR joins them.*

DOCTOR Are you getting a lift into town?
MICHEL Matvey's driving me.
DOCTOR Because I should be able to do the needful later in the day. (*Softly*) In a brand-new troika — azure blue!
MICHEL You're a real rogue — you know that?
DOCTOR Me! (*Hand on heart*) My entire life is dedicated to the sick and the poor, Michel.

*And he explodes with laughter.*

MICHEL Goodbye, everybody. I'm off. 'Bye. 'Bye. 'Bye.

*He quickly shakes several hands.*

'Bye, Lizaveta.
LIZAVETA Safe journey, Michel.
SCHAAF Travel in health.
MICHEL Thank you. Anna — goodbye.
ANNA Any time you feel like coming back.
ARKADY He knows that, Mother. Come on — I'll see you off.
DOCTOR We both will.

*General goodbyes, and MICHEL, ARKADY and the DOCTOR leave.*

SCHAAF Michel is a good man. Already I am lonely for him. My eyes they wish to wet.

ANNA You mean to — Oh, damn!

LIZAVETA *takes out her snuff-box.*

Lizaveta!

LIZAVETA (*Innocently*) Yes?

ANNA What are you doing?

LIZAVETA I am snuffing.

ANNA I will not have you indulge that filthy habit in this house, Lizaveta.

LIZAVETA Then I'll have to say goodbye to this house, won't I?

SCHAAF 'Bye! Another 'Bye! Mein Gott!

ANNA And what does that mean?

LIZAVETA Another 'Bye indeed, Herr Schaaf. In three weeks to be exact!

SCHAAF And who stay? Nobody — nobody — nobody!

*Enter* MATVEY *and* KATYA *with tea-trays. They are both beaming and move almost in tandem.*

MATVEY Sorry we're a bit late.

KATYA Not altogether our fault.

MATVEY Tea for everybody?

KATYA We have coffee, too.

MATVEY Katya has made some delicious crumpets.

KATYA Matvey!

MATVEY They're wonderful.

KATYA Don't listen to him. They're simple drop scones.

ANNA Bring everything out to the lawn, Katya.

KATYA My pleasure, Madam. After you.

*They all move outside except* MATVEY *who tidies the drawing-room. Music: Nocturne No. 9 in E-flat major.* BOLSHINTSOV *enters — smiling, uneasy, nervous.*

BOLSHINTSOV Matvey.

MATVEY Ah! You gave me a start. Sir?

BOLSHINTSOV I'm looking for Doctor Shpigelsky.

MATVEY Certainly. I'll get him. He's somewhere around.

BOLSHINTSOV  No, no; don't disturb him. Just tell him I've left the
            horses and the trap at the back gate.

MATVEY  I'll do that. Can I get you something? Tea? Coffee?

BOLSHINTSOV  Nothing, thanks. Is that Miss Vera?

MATVEY  That's Miss Vera. Terrific, isn't she?

> BOLSHINTSOV, *his face raised, stands listening, smiling.*

BOLSHINTSOV  Nice ... nice ...

> MATVEY *exits with his tray. The music continues for
> a few seconds; then stops abruptly in mid-phrase.*
> BOLSHINTSOV *stands there, his face raised, still
> smiling, waiting.*